The Non-Crucifixion of Jesus

by

Ahmed Ismail

Order this book online at www.trafford.com/08-0763
or email orders@trafford.com

Most Trafford titles are also available at major online book retailers.

Note for Librarians: A cataloguing record for this book is available from Library and Archives Canada at www.collectionscanada.ca/amicus/index-e.html

ISBN: 978-1-4251-8080-5

We at Trafford believe that it is the responsibility of us all, as both individuals and corporations, to make choices that are environmentally and socially sound. You, in turn, are supporting this responsible conduct each time you purchase a Trafford book, or make use of our publishing services. To find out how you are helping, please visit www.trafford.com/responsiblepublishing.html

Our mission is to efficiently provide the world's finest, most comprehensive book publishing service, enabling every author to experience success. To find out how to publish your book, your way, and have it available worldwide, visit us online at www.trafford.com/10510

www.trafford.com

North America & international
toll-free: 1 888 232 4444 (USA & Canada)
phone: 250 383 6864 ♦ fax: 250 383 6804 ♦ email: info@trafford.com

The United Kingdom & Europe
phone: +44 (0)1865 722 113 ♦ local rate: 0845 230 9601
facsimile: +44 (0)1865 722 868 ♦ email: info.uk@trafford.com

10 9 8 7 6 5 4 3 2 1

CONTENTS

INTRODUCTION

To suggest a position of re-thinking the crucifixion scenario, as most people of a non-Islamic faith would understand it, would seem a little bit bizarre. Both Jews and Christians believe and have a history to prove their beliefs that Jesus the son of Mary was in fact crucified. They even have an uncomfortable understanding with each other about this event. That is, the reason why he was crucified. While one side of the coin has pigeonholed this event as getting rid of an imposter and therefore a dealer in deceptions or at best a man who was deluded into thinking he was something that he was not, another side attributes this event as being the heralding of great and glorious news for salvation and the forgiveness of sins.

As an aside to these varied beliefs comes the comforting thought of 'blame it on the Romans' for the Roman soldiers grabbed this soon to be 'crucified' individual and the rest is supposed to be history. Well, go right ahead and blame the Romans. They are extinct and cannot defend themselves and that makes for a perfect fall guy and for peaceful coexistence between the two groups—the Jews and those who call themselves Christians.

Between these two mighty groups of people who claim to study from the same book, the Bible, come thoughts about this man who they claim as the one who was crucified. That so-called crucified man is thought of in a wide range of belief. He is thought of as being a charlatan, an imposter, a trouble making upstart, a good man and a prophet, a god and finally an offspring of God. In fact, some people declare that he is both god and a man practically at the same time. It is no wonder that people have come to blows over this idea. So there you are!

It seems that an impartial referee would find too much variation going on here especially if one has a continuity of records called Holy Books as deemed as guides for the flock. That shows quite clearly that people are confused and have not quite come to grips with a common understanding. It is true that groups X and Y have a right to exist but X and Y seem to, at times, mix together like oil and water. And what keeps them apart? The same thing that should join them together—Religion.

Do the common believers know much about their religions? The answer is no they do not. I am not talking about the performance of rituals but the essence of religion and not one being born into a particular religion. However, there are, thank God, people who seem to have a natural tendency to just be kind and compassionate no matter their faith and are less prone to get offensive about issues they feel are written in stone.

For the Christian, the idea that Jesus was crucified is normal. Throughout the history of this topic, legends and legendary personalities have grown up to espouse great and marvelous wonders proclaiming such philosophical nonsense that it only seemed sense to add onto the legend and create a multi-layered story all by itself. The truth about the crucifixion matter is quite a tale in itself.

While many are led to believe that the crucifixion story has been outright clear from the beginning in that a total consensus about this issue has been understood from day one, the truth of the matter is quite different. While it is true that the vast majority of this issue has been lost as well as other issues, most Christians would maintain that the records found in the New Testament/Old Testament speak for themselves.

In a way they do but if only these issues are well understood across the board from all accredited religious records. Can anyone in today's world actually be taken seriously, who states, "My God is better than your God?" Just the very definition of the word 'God' and what that represents in any language is enough to call the bluff of any buffoon who would believe their 'God' is better than The God. That is why the use of the total accredited religious records is necessary.

Another reason to include <u>all</u> the records is that one has to reject flippancy and incorporate seriousness. That is that one should try to understand that certain sayings found in scripture might have a different meaning than what is commonly believed and these things must be checked and cross-referenced as much as possible.

A good reason to be careful when researching any particular point is to be practical and intelligent about one's source of information and not foolish. If the source is believed to be perfect, then one should say so and be in a position to prove it. However, proof does not come from ideological grounds but from factual scholarly evidence.

Once over these hurdles it must be understood that people have an inalienable right to believe as they want to believe and are only responsible in earthly terms to the sect/religious viewpoints to which they belong. For example, a Roman

Catholic does not have to follow or believe in the beliefs of the Muslims, Jews or Protestants. In fact, a person does not have to believe anything at all on the religious front but all true religions do talk about a person's accountability or Judgment in the afterlife. What a person does with it is his business as long as he refrains from breaking the laws of the land and enters not forcibly into areas that by consensus have been closed to him. That means that a polite refusal from one party to refrain from discussion is on their heads and that is that! So let that be thrown into the mix.

Jewish and Christian ideologies have tended to clash very dramatically over the man called Jesus throughout the centuries. There is no need to recount the dirt thrown up by both sides and the torment caused by these things. However, the Jews have always managed to get the Christian's goat by reminding them that since Jesus was a Jew and never heard of Christianity and because he as a Jew overstepped his bounds, he received his just desserts. That message was always implied and that tended to infuriate the Christians, because according to Christian thinking, a person had to be abnormal to refuse to look a gift horse in the mouth.

This attitude led to persecution and demeaning of a people who maintained that they had their own way of doing things. Hence, it was understood by implied actions that the 'grand reformer', for want of a better term, was to be treated as a total bust according to one side. In other words, the feeling became prevalent that the Jews preferred to ignore this man called Jesus as somewhat irrelevant. Perhaps it would have been better for the Christian to say, "Suit yourself" and keep it at that but the world doesn't work that way.

So blaming defenseless Romans is like a murderer blaming the devil and wanting the devil put on death row instead of himself. Well the world sometimes turns like that also.

False Gnosticism was around centuries before the emergence of Jesus the son of Mary and historically it caused a great deal of trouble to the budding church. The church was told not to mix the leaven with the lump but it went ahead on its own course and did so. The so-called writings of Paul and even John do contain many Gnostic elements within them and that is ok because they had a foundation within their ideas. But after the death of the original Apostles and their companions (true followers) unscrupulous individuals came into the church and spread false doctrine and confusion. What seems to be even worse than that is what occurred after 100 AC.

After this admittedly conjectural date, there arose individuals who chose to go into combating false Gnosticism by seemingly creating some of their own peculiar explanations. It was as if they were fighting fire with fire.

The success of Christ's fundamental teachings were subverted to more interesting things like the explanation of the meaning of the Word and pigeonholing it into a Christian dogma to counteract the foolishness of the false Gnostics. The false Gnostics had their explanations that amounted to nothing more than strange Eastern doggerel further mixed up with pagan doctrine heralding the new Way that included an explanation of Jesus the Christ. Therefore, it became like a contest between paganism and real Christianity and in the minds of those philosophers and corrupt thinkers in the church, they were ready to delve into areas that were so far over their heads that they made Christianity look paganish in certain ways.

These things did not happen overnight but slowly evolved until a real devil was to sit on the throne and let the 'children of ignorance' play out their little dramas. And we do know who that person was as well as some of his characteristics and the character of some of his sycophants who were members of the church in 'good standing'.

After the damage was done, the horses could not be put back in the barn but that did not stop Christianity from being a viable and helpful religion to those who wanted to get away from the fanfare of philosophical debates and just lead lives of the remembrance of Jesus. But that wasn't going to be easy when the church ruled the day. History is littered with examples of church foolishness that put people under hard constraints for their own personal gain. Islam, the Protestant Reformation and science came along and the church had to rethink some of its positions and have its ego deflated.

And it is not only the church that had to undergo a new way of thinking. Every religion and every age has shown difficulties and peculiar philosophies that had nothing whatsoever to do with its founder. For example, the great intellect and reformer, Ibn Taymiyah, came up against a multitude of philosophical junk spread by half-baked Sufis who were wrecking Islam. Ibn Taymiyah, who understood real Sufism and its rarity, but who was primarily an excellent scholar, undertook a period of reform against those who tried to tarnish Islam. The result was that Islam could defend itself from within and without based on common sense rather than fluffy philosophy.

Now we come to another Pandora's Box called the crucifixion. This historical moneymaker has also put more people in their graves than people would care to think about. Is it possible that men of good faith can actually follow the precedence of good faith? Can men of maturity arise and take a mature look at things without having a crisis of ego? If man is to spiritually advance, then that is what he will have to do!

A DIP INTO HISTORY

The Catholic faith has always stood its ground in expostulating the so-called 'true faith'. Its roots, they claim, extend all the way back to an unbroken line of bishops of Rome thus giving a historical chain of true apostolic fathers. But is that really the case? In truth, this case is overblown, misused and completely out of touch with reality. It is true that there is a historical chain of papal rulers but a deep look into actual events and theological snafus leads one to question this 'divine right of kings' philosophy. This inflexibility of the 'true' church would lead to the death of tens of millions of individuals who maintained that they were Christians as well as others who were not Christians.

Forgoing the religion of Islam and Judaism for the moment, the development of Protestantism threw a spanner into the works of Roman Catholicism. Protestantism flourished because it wanted scriptural insights rather than philosophical mumbo-jumbo. In other words, it became a rule of thumb to hold to the scriptures rather than go off into a tangent of fairytales produced by 'great' thinkers who spoke often but knew even less.

However, the Protestants were in for a surprise. It seems that it is almost in the nature of man to wonder about nonsensical bilge and foolish things and leave the importance of life behind. Therefore, the Protestants ended up in forming a multitude of various and contradictory sects arguing about superfluous details that only half-baked people would consider important. The big lesson here is that by getting away from scripture and turning to the philosophers, one can literally pollute real faith.

The Roman Catholics meanwhile continue to hold the ace of historical events up their sleeve and while hoping that no one should take a close look at some of their champions from the past, are happy to go about business as usual.

Sometimes, even unwittingly, it is these heroes who helped in destroying real Christianity even when their intensions were to save it and amazingly enough Biblical prophecy goes on to explain in part how they were going to accomplish it!

Some of these characters from church history that had a large impact on its future development as to belief systems were as follows:

1. Justin Martyr
2. Tertullian
3. Montanus
4. Constantine

How could they accomplish such things? In part, they elevated their organization to such a degree that it seemed a miracle to be blessed to be a part of that whole. Therefore, happy is the man who has been elevated above his brother—the unfortunate one who is not a member of that faith or philosophy. That concept does not form the basis of any true religion although in truth it does sort of <u>shadow</u> real belief. But it is a fake imitation of correct principles laid down in the real scriptures and like high class counterfeit money, it is not easy to spot by the unwary.

Hence, many people can be taken for a ride because their knowledge of their own faith is made of straw and not steel. So faith and the indulgence in faith is a job in itself which many of the flocks around the world woefully neglect thus proving that man can try and live by bread alone although that has never been suggested in any scripture.

One such character from church history was Justin Martyr. Born a pagan around 100 AC and a dabbler in what best can be called pagan/Christian philosophy, this converted 'Catholic' crusader loved to wow his listeners with philosophical mumbo-jumbo. Three of his biggest contributions in church history were to cement the idea, for the last time, concerning the crucifixion of Jesus, his so-called divinity and his relationship to the One God. Besides the crucifixion issue his big contributions were to set forth Jesus as a real son of the living God and his last contribution was to set forth arguments for the interpretation of the 'Logos' concept which eventually was to lead others to the pathway of explaining how Jesus was somehow related to the Divine. In truth, he had no business discussing the subject of 'Logos' but if one goes into ancient history one might be able to understand why he attempted it.

Acceptable religion has been with humanity since its entrance into Earth. There has also followed in the wake of true religion that which was false or what one can call paganism. Paganism has formed different offshoots just as religion has had different offshoots. Paganism has its own system of gods, sons of gods, creation theories and various levels of mythical inventions. Paganism was around long before the entrance of Jesus the son of Mary (pbh) and each sect had its own priest-class to explain the mysteries of the universal creation.

Even though Christianity was a growing concern in the pagan world during Paul's time, it still had to battle for the hearts and minds of the people. A lot of those people seemed to fancy the notion of myths and false mysticism which probably to them added color to their lives. Christianity, in being sensible and forthright, did not seem to have quite as much color or as much as a circus atmosphere as did pagan beliefs and customs. Christianity's central figure, Jesus the Messiah, was perhaps a little too bland for the people who were hell-bent on looking for colorful fairytales.

The concept of what was called 'Logos' was not a new term in philosophical circles as well as pagan circles and various offbeat theories were presented to explain it. The 'church' was not to be found lacking in this extracurricular activity either. Well, Justin Martyr gave his rendition of what he believed the Logos to be, thus opening the door for Christianity to match the wonders of circus-like paganism.

In the Quran we find a statement concerning what philosophers down through the centuries have tried to decipher:

And they ask you (O Muhammad) concerning the Ruh (the Spirit); Say, "The Ruh (Spirit) is one of the things, the knowledge of which is only with my Lord. And of knowledge you (mankind) have been given only a little." Q (17: 85)

The lesson here should be to let things that cannot be understood left alone. The philosophers, like Justin Martyr, sometime ignore this good advice and in the end lead others astray in search of wild fantasies strictly condemned in all of the religious records.

Concerning the so-called crucifixion, Justin Martyr became the 'voice' of the church in Rome when in about 148 AC, he finalized the debate about whether Jesus was actually crucified or not. According to his research, Jesus was most definitely crucified and one must not overlook that Martyr did do research. The question to ask would be what kind of research did he do?

In order to find the 'truth', Justin Martyr went to the Jews as well as falling back on ancient Roman records. He did not like the Jews (remember that this is 148 AC and Christianity was rising its head against the condemners of Christ—philosophically anyways) but he wanted to find out if they really believed that they had killed Jesus. Their answer, of course, was that they killed the imposter and that was that. As for the Romans, they had records and as worldly people, they took down what they saw. Religious miracles were not their forte. The Romans were as worldly as one gets and mostly they depended on paganism.

Whatever the case, Justin Martyr had his so-called proof which seemed solid enough and he was not going to be silenced by what he would claim as spurious documents claiming otherwise. In other words, Jesus was crucified because he was crucified and that was going to be that!

Another stalwart of future Catholic fame was Tertullian born around 160 AC. Tertullian is an amazing study because of his lack of being canonized by the Church in Rome. That is amazing since his contributions to Roman Catholicism cannot be overemphasized. This one-time pagan turned Christian/philosopher/apologist and lawyer had few peers when it came to oratory and persuasion.

His noteworthy productions include the strongest defense for the church of Rome going back into history noting the passing of the torch from Jesus to his Apostles to the true line of 'popes'. This established the great link of continuation of perfect and unassailable linkage whereby church authority could not be questioned. This act was done to counter all false ideas whose pagan origins could not be shown to have such great depth or lineage. In other words, with such a pedigree the church wins easily against all comers (ideas—pagan or Gnostic because they could not show their rightful beginnings). So it becomes logical that when they want to express something new and wonderful, they could not go back to original sources. Therefore, their expressions were nothing but fluff and inventions.

The second brilliant coup was coming up with the term 'Trinitus' in explaining the beginning philosophical notion of a form of 3 Gods in one idea. Although Tertullian did not quite get that far, he laid the groundwork for other goofy philosophers to come along and build on his foundations. He also was a firm believer in the crucifixion of Christ, which the church has held as an unshakeable truth. However, he adds a new twist to that idea. According to Tertullian, the only reason that Jesus should have undergone that humiliation was because of certain vermin placed on this earth. The real cause of why Jesus had to be crucified was simple. It was because of that sinful and disgraceful other half of humanity called women. This ingenious philosopher seems to have a flair for overstatement as he places the guilt of the human race and the reason why Jesus had to die squarely on the shoulders of what he considered as vermin—women! It follows logically that when one goes into his history that this man became an overzealous ascetic who had little regard for the fairer sex.

After his death, for nearly a century, Tertullian became a kind of forgotten slug, whose name was not mentioned much. However, after that period his name comes once more into vogue as a chief architect and builder of the great Roman Church. One might wonder why this eloquent and dynamic thinker was not only boycotted for a time but was never canonized by the institution he so vehemently defended.

The big reason for his lack of sainthood is simple. He died a heretic. The same church that he defended with such 'eloquence' just could not stand his next brilliant move, which landed him in hot water and the brand of being a heretic. Along came a man called Montanus, who is sometimes considered the father of modern of Pentecostalism, and Tertullian followed and praised him eagerly.

This 'solid' Christian activist started his movement around 167-170 AC and was to cause a huge uproar in Christian circles that it is no doubt that both Christians and Muslims would agree to Montanus being one of the little anti-christs of his day. He was a Christian and well steeped in Christianity but he also was a very dangerous person as his ideas spread like wildfire throughout the Christian empire of the day. His movement gained a lot of momentum, which shows that Christianity was <u>not</u> a solid and unified religion except for the centralized church in Rome.

This ascetic man accompanied by two woman friends, Priscilla and Maximilla, started to openly declare that they were getting direct revelations from the Holy Spirit (Gabriel) who anointed him as That Prophet or the spirit of truth incarnated in the flesh. In other words, he openly declared that he was the Paraclete spoken about in the Gospel of John.

In Islamic terms that would mean he would be announcing himself as Prophet Muhammad.

His declarations had such a profound effect on the church at Rome that even Pope Eleutherus has been recorded to have written letters in favor of Montanism. However, there was a change in mood amongst the Roman church as it became evident that the institution of popedom as well as the church in Rome would become in grave danger. Therefore, the letters of praise by Pope Eleutherus, the so-called Vicar of Christ on Earth, were hastily recalled. Needless to say, eventually the so-called Christian charlatan Montanus and the new Christianity that he preached eventually after several decades of huge success ended up on the garbage heap where it belonged.

As for Tertullian, the church maintains that he saw the error of his ways and returned to the body of the church towards the end of his life but this has never been proven.

One bright spot going for the church at about this time comes from Irenaeus. Hardly anything is known about his life but he does hold an important spot in church history. Irenaeus was not a philosopher nor was he much of a theologian. He was more of a historian and peacemaker. It is known from history that he opposed Gnosticism with great vigor. One of his strong suits was in having a tenuous relationship with Polycarp in his youth resulting in sort of a continuum of religious thinking.

The importance of Irenaeus lies in his historical research into church history and in his writings of the occurrences that were happening in his day and somewhat of a history to those heretical sects of Christianity. From Irenaeus, a true champion of orthodoxy, we learn that Christianity was definitely not as stable a religion as people are led to believe but was constantly in a state of flux with many different types of philosophies.

When it came down to writing about the earliest decades of true Christianity, Irenaeus was not on solid ground. In fact, he had to depend upon oral traditions handed down by the 'church fathers' and fill in the huge gaps that were missing as best as he could. His research did help to stabilize the acceptable books of the New Testament and although his list of acceptable books does not tally exactly as what is found in the New Testament of today, it is close enough. Irenaeus was not a maker of doctrine nor was he an eloquent speaker but that did not matter. He gave a history that provided a much-needed foundation to make the church more credible. So, thanks to the historian Irenaeus, we have a more fundamental look at the foolishness that was happening in the land of the Christian/pagan Empire.

It took nearly a century after Irenaeus but Christianity was on the move big time in the Roman Empire. Paganism was still a viable force but it was losing its grip upon the people. However, doctrinal debate was still rife within the church and for decades the church was arguing over the true nature of the Messiah and it was about to come to a head in the Arian debates. Enter now one of the lofty saints of the Catholic Church but to others a crafty demon. The man was Constantine.

History and the actions of Constantine go on to show exactly what kind of man he really was and it becomes readily apparent why the Catholic Church considers this individual a great saint.

In truth, Constantine did not care one whit for Jesus or anything Christian and this is proved by his 'conversion' to Christianity only on his deathbed. In fact, this creature was a cold calculating individual who thought only for himself. It is true that he was a worshiper of the Cross and a follower of a god called the 'sun god' but that goes on to show that he was an outright pagan. But who said pagans couldn't be crafty and deep thinking?

Constantine was a man driven to lead an empire and the quickest way to get what he wanted was to unite a divided people under one banner—his own. History paints this man as a somewhat ruthless character that inspired an aura of awe, fear and respect. In his personal march to fame, he found out the realities of life soon enough. Paganism was on the wane but Christianity through various methods was on the increase and growing stronger by the day. It was a force of belief to be reckoned with and it was a force that would clearly dominate the political scene. Therefore, it had to be addressed carefully. In the past, tormenting the Christians made them stronger and not weaker. If this new 'philosophy' was going to overtake paganism, then that was the force that Constantine would use to get his empire.

Unfortunately, the Christians were having this several decades old confrontation amongst themselves as to whom Jesus really was. This was not going to get Constantine his beloved united empire filled with disenfranchised Christians. So being already known as a Christian supporter (for his own designs) he threatened the church to become organized or else. He also, like the crafty devil he was, gave all the expectations of making the new and approved doctrines these 'bishops' would come up with as the only way and means of worship. It is the old idea of 'you get what you want without interference from me and I'll get what I want without interference from you'. It was to turn out to be a happy marriage. Remember, by his fruits you will know him and that sentiment is from the New Testament itself.

Constantine could not care less if Jesus was regulated to a god or a piece of cheese. That was not his concern because truth and religion were not his concern. When the Arian Controversy was over and the dust settled, Christianity in around 325 AC became primarily what it is today concerning doctrine.

To show pleasure with their new leader or what would be called kissing his feet in today's world, the high church decided to honor this 'devil' with fawning flatteries—just to cement their relationship with this powerful dictator and to be blessed in his presence.

It was reckoned that Christianity must have a symbol to celebrate this victory. In fact, it already had one (the fish) but why stop there? Constantine must be flattered and so the new symbol must reflect the greatness of this man. The new symbol became the Cross—a symbol very close to Constantine's still pagan heart. And to add a little bit more sweetener to the pot, the sun god's birthday which is around December 25th would be exactly Jesus' birthday. WOW! What a coincidence. People should spend some time dwelling on that idea as to what it means to be a toady to some powerful figure like Constantine and the history of the church.

As to his conversion to Christianity on his deathbed, that idea seems to be psychologically explainable. Much like the Pharaohs of old who needed to establish monuments for their worship or the presidents of today who make libraries as symbols of their reigns on Earth, Constantine had thrown his weight behind Christianity and not paganism. So who could blame Constantine for wanting to be remembered as king of kings, emperor of emperors, giants among men, leader of leaders amongst the faithful, chosen of God, and conqueror of the known universe. What a legacy this buffoon was building for himself! He sure was not going to get the pagan vote so it is logical to see why he, of such staunch defense of true faith and fear of the One God, finally caved in and became a Christian on his deathbed.

This is where the Cross becomes the central thrust for Christianity. This does not mean that the Cross was not a part of Christianity in the past but it now becomes even bigger than Jesus (pbh). Therefore, from philosophical to political development which is not hidden when true history is looked at, one can get the real picture, a clearer picture as to the dynamics of how a religion can be kidnapped and manipulated not so much by one man but by people willing to toady up to this creature of ill repute called the false priest-class.

The concept of the cross appears to be an evolutionary one that has a basis in fact. There was a crucifixion and that is a certainty. However, where does the notion of the crucifixion of Jesus precisely begin? That is somewhat of a mystery that can be almost possible to trace. Many of the Jews at the time of the actual crucifixion event from the Pharisaical sect would have believed that Jesus was actually crucified and would carry this tale for their own glorification of being the legitimate defenders of the truth.

Adding to the confusion of this myth would be the philosopher/pagan mixed bag of tricks that eagerly hung on to the legend of Jesus and proclaimed his triumph over flesh and hence the grave by having him being one of the 'divines' or sons of a central god- type legend. Their big time show was to incriminate the regular 'bums' of this earth in the presence of one who is of a super race of beings. Hence, when they went to grab this man who was not a real man, what they grabbed was nothing but spirit. Therefore, how could anyone crucify a spirit that had no corporeal body?

It is found in the New Testament, however, that these criminals who infested the church early on would make such false accusations which turned truth into a comic sideshow and thus they (those false Christian philosophers/Gnostics) were condemned as being wolves in sheep's clothing or little anti-christs. The epistles of John and the Acts help to fill us in on these events but do not mention much beyond that.

In order to combat the idea of the ethereal Jesus, a man of spirit but no flesh, it seemed logical to have him become an actual partaker of the crucifixion itself. And those who did so could feel justified by certain passages of the Old Testament and manuscripts purporting to be various writings from the followers of Jesus as well as from the writings of Paul. This too is covered in the present day New Testament especially by Peter who writes about Paul being a good brother but one who is very difficult to understand at times. That is not all. He also puts the blame on those who are half-witted and who twist meanings of Biblical context out of all due proportion.

So we can see that the church is going to face some real heavy hitters who will become their enemies and actually cause a great deal of disruption to the body of believers. This body of believers is not going to live forever and after approximately 82-85 AC who is left who can counteract the poison being spread? The answer is not many will be left and certainly not in Rome.

Besides this, the idea of a physical crucifixion of Jesus is a lot easier to defend than a Jesus who was not crucified which sounds like the church would be falling into the Gnostic hands again with no way out of this quagmire. The phony Gnostics could now lick their wounds and fiddle with their *Gospel of Judas* and other phony gospels and have devils arise from the dust like Basilides who tried to peddle a new version of Christianity to the world. That, however, was not going to work and even though the truth was being diluted, the sense that Christianity was still hanging in there against all odds was nothing short of a miracle.

The devil does not sleep and go away so easily. He keeps hammering away at the problem until he pollutes just about every stream coming from the river. Once the door is opened, the horses will bolt from the barn and now it becomes everyman for himself. And this can be seen from the foolishness of Justin Martyr on up with very few exceptions. Give the devil his due but he still is an idiot and he cannot control the events of time and space. He can't stop those of brave hearts from actually thinking or from those desiring to love the One God. All he can do is try to make life uncomfortable for people who care. He also cannot stop people from thinking or choosing and people who think actually pose quite a danger to him and his group—the other beasts as in Jinn and corrupt men.

There is one thing that these beasts could not do and that was to take away the Old and New Testaments in their entirety. Nor could they stop the behavior of men to do deeds of righteousness and character building. The only damage they could do was to themselves and those who are attracted to such immoral creeds built on philosophical nonsense.

A lesson here can be learned from the lowly maggot. Doctors use maggots at times in hospitals to eat away dead and dieing tissue. Notice that the maggots will not eat or go for healthy tissue. So what does that mean? It means that man moves according to (follows) his own disposition as stated in the Quran. And if certain things appeal to certain individuals, then that is what they will follow.

THE NON-CRUCIFIXION OF JESUS

The idea that Jesus the son of Mary (pbh) was not crucified and that he was not put on the cross and that he did not die is a contentious issue between Jews, Christians and Muslims. Yet the One God of all the sons of Adam has given us the answer and people still want to wrangle over the idea.

Allah made things clear and unambiguous in His Word, which is true. However, people, instead of listening to His Word, have by their own dispositions, become unmindful to reality and seek what their own hearts contain. Therefore, yet another prophecy has come true. The warnings given by the prophets to stay on the straight path and not to wander off it seems to be ignored.

At the end of this piece, I will, Allah Willing, provide documentation for most of the things said according to scripture that I used.

It is also a great sadness to see (according to the Internet featuring 'Muslim beliefs' from Wikipedia) that so much contention about this issue has arisen amongst so-called Muslim sects. Perhaps this piece of writing might help solve some of the problems facing these so-called sects of Islam—As Allah Wills.

Still, humanity caught in its own morass seeks to try to understand what at first seems to be the unreachable or the hopelessness of the case. To top things off, we are told in the Quran to go and seek out knowledge. That is, we are told to try to understand the world we live in rather than act like mere robots. But even this has been clarified so as to bring the seeker home safely. To seek out knowledge for knowledge sake is lunacy. To seek out knowledge that is the right kind of knowledge, the knowledge that does well rather than harm and the knowledge that glorifies Allah is acceptable. Although knowledge is good, it can be destructive and very bad for the human being. This has been proven repeatedly throughout history when certain knowledge has been abused.

When a person seeks out knowledge, especially of a religious nature, it is incumbent upon that person to be extremely careful and honest. If he cannot do so or if there is crookedness in his heart, then he will be answerable for it and punished heavily for it. This is especially true in religious matters!

When discussing religious matters like 'comparative religion' or even one's own religion, there are some <u>ground rules</u> that cannot be overlooked. This is especially true of certain apparent conflicts between 'the religions' or what is known by Muslims as The People of the Book. Some of these ground rules are as follows:

1. Allah rules, not the person's ego. Therefore, seek out His Guidance and Protection.

2. Follow His Prophet's direction and try not to go beyond it.
3. Use one's common sense but understand that Allah has set limits to all things.
4. Never, under any circumstance go against the first line of defense of Truth. The first line of defense for Muslims is the Glorious Quran, which is full, complete and totally accurate right down to every letter and the placement thereof. That is, anything conflicting with this greatest and truthfulness of written Word is false.
5. The importance of life is SALVATION and not mystery unraveling and Allah Sees all that we do. So, by implication, the following of His Prophet's commands, actions and deeds (as much as one is able) is a sure way of attaining Paradise and removal from falsehoods.

One cannot study anything in a vacuum, so the idea of 'comparative religion' is needed to study the idea of the non-crucifixion of Jesus (pbh) under the idea of getting to know the People of the Book—only. That is, the Muslims have all that they need to know or what is important to know and do not have to go beyond that point. However, to make it clear to them concerning the matter and also to give them, with Allah's Permission only, a chance and a choice to open their eyes or make it known about their stubbornness to Revelation let them decide for there is no compulsion in religion!

The 'Heart' of the matter lies in the trust of Allah (God). That is true faith. So, the heart of the matter now becomes the Quran. Is the Quran perfect and has it been perfectly preserved? The answer, which looks too complex for human beings to answer, actually is very simple. Several steps are needed to examine the issue just to see where real faith belongs:

1. The first step must come from the human side—that is the reality of whether Prophet Muhammad (pbh) is for real! There are two ways to look at this problem. Looking at what he did and looking at what was foretold about him if anything. This 'bringing forth the evidence' is justified so a look through the literature of the Peoples of the Book as well as the oldest manuscripts of the Hindu faith can give us a clue as to, when and where he shall be born and what his station is, if the records can be believed.
2. The second thing one should understand is that if he is going to be accredited with a Holy Book, what does he say about this Book?
3. The third point is to find out what that Book says about itself.

To shorten matters the claim is that the Quran is 100% accurate down to the last arranged letter and that no falsehoods have crept into that Book. This idea is obtained as to its truthfulness by two basic ways: evidence that is internal and evidence that is external. Internal evidence is what is found in the Book itself (what it says about itself), the culture that took care of that book as to its characteristics and if one can find the very earliest copy of that book. This has been gone into many times before and books have been written about this aspect. The external evidence would come from an outside source or manuscript such as the Old or New Testament. God declares that the truthfulness of this Book can be found in the scriptures of the People of the Book—Q (Sura 26: 196) (1).

The last statement is surprising to many but it is true. In the surviving Old Testament, in Zephaniah, Chapter 3 verses 9 and 10 (2), the declaration of the Quran as a pure religious type of language will be given to a nation of peoples who seemingly have been forgotten and that their prayer lines will be taken very seriously such that they will take care to maintain a straight line standing shoulder to shoulder in prayer. Obviously, God did not forget the Arabs but the prophets rained down upon the Jews like a storm and the Arabs were seemingly out of it. In addition, the Arabic language is not pure at all and neither is any other language because they keep changing. However, a pure religious language does exist and that would be called 'Quranic Arabic'. Moreover, Arabia is the land across from Ethiopia.

Now that this point has been clarified, one can now turn towards this Book and find out exactly what one should think about the other claimed books from the People of the Book—Jews and Christians.

It is not what we are supposed to invent. What precisely does Allah tell us about their records? Then, having established Allah's advice, one should go to the Prophet and seek his council. What did he have to say about these things and what did he show if anything that is valuable to us. That may be a long story but his chief saying is important. The People of the Book are classified as to being Children of Israel and this makes sense when one understands that Jesus (pbh) was the last of the Israeli prophets. Later, at some point in time, the newly reformed Jews (those who believed and acted in good faith towards their prophet Jesus) declared themselves Christians but still we are interested in ancient times and not modern classifications.

So, what gives? What gives is the fact that the Prophet was very clear about what to do. He declared that it is OK to listen to stories about these people (Jews and Christians) but not to give a definite yes or no to their stories or sayings. Of course, if what they say agrees totally with the 'Pure Book' well that is all right.

Man can use his God-given logic and understanding but he should not go overboard and randomly pick and choose what he wants to believe in. He has to be extremely careful and in no case should he ever knowingly contradict what is in the pure, Holy Book—the Quran.

What we can fathom from the Old Testament, Dead Sea Scrolls and the New Testament is that they suffer from some grave defects but they still have the weight of truth in them. We know this because Allah has implied that those people (Jews and Christians) can still study their own records and find the truth but, except for a few, they do not study their own records carefully. In fact, they tend to go to their religious guides and let them decide. It would be hard to go to non-existent records to find any truth. So, with that in mind, and taking all due precaution, the story of Jesus' non-crucifixion can be, if not trusted in all its aspects, then looked at with a new light. For of a surety, the Pure Word of Allah states it quite succinctly: Jesus was neither on the cross nor was he killed but it was made to appear unto the people that he was being crucified and those who dwell on the subject are full of gnawing doubts—except those who trust in the Pure Word and Allah's Prophet. That is a paraphrased statement to be sure but the essentials are there.

Therefore, man being curious, sometimes foolhardy, and often hasty would like to know what did happen. Believe it or not, we get all we need to know about that matter from Allah. Still, people keep yammering for clarification. Most of them talk like empty barrels and the more clarification given, the less they will believe. However, some may believe and by Allah's Will and only by His Will, will they have their eyes opened.

Muslims find that the Old and New Testaments contain several interesting but dangerous traits:

1. Words have been altered from the original source. Some words have been changed in spelling but look almost the same as the original form.

2. Words have also been substituted for the original words. That is, a completely new unrelated word has been used in place of the original.

3. Time sequences are sometimes out of balance. For example, what Jesus might have said during his first year of ministry now appears at the end of his ministry. It is not that what is reported is wrong but the understanding may be off as its context is messed up.

4. The last point happens to deal with human feelings. It is not a mystery that certain people due to fear, jealousy, pride, arrogance and or ignorance feel that they somehow own or secretly possess God. That is, that through love of self, their 'god' would think and do like them. Therefore, their god is greater than your god based on financial, national, scriptural interpretations, and personal thought and they will not or can't listen to the One God of all the sons of Adam because that would sort of level the playing field.

Hence, by a kinky way of seemingly controlling their 'god' by worshiping him, he puts them in a sort of elevated condition of great glory as opposed to others. Talking to these people would be like talking to a stone and indeed the Muslim understands this when reading the Quran—Q (Sura 25: 44) (3). It may be part of immature humanity to seek favoritism but this so-called favoritism is shown in its true light by the saying of the Prophet as to who really is the best of people who are on the right way.

The Story of the Supposed Crucifixion of Jesus the son of Mary

There is no simple way to start this story so I will just start it and let it take its course and then at various points I will, as Allah Wills, try to decipher the story into understandable parts. Mostly, this part will feature the Christian viewpoint with only slight variations. Latter a mostly Muslim viewpoint will be presented with some slight variations.

The first thing to point out is that there is a difference between being an intimate Companion of Jesus (of which he had 12) and a disciple of Jesus of which he had several thousand. History discuses the Essenic sect, which was the third most populace of Jewish sects and who were enemies of the Pharisaical sect, or the largest of the sects of Jews. History also points out that Jesus performed many miracles and people were aware of his goodness and that he was in no way a renegade or liar.

Even a hadith in Bukhari states that after Lot (Lut) Allah gave strong support to His prophets so in this way we know that Jesus had a somewhat large following of people consisting of those strong in belief to those weak in belief.

His special disciples (Companions) were those who ate and slept with him and they accompanied him throughout his mission. The other 'believers' would be his followers as to his teachings or discipline and because of that they would be called disciples. In the Quran we find the story of the 'Youths of the Cave' and see that after several hundred years after Jesus (pbh) he still had 'disciples' or believers in him. However, after the youths went to sleep in one era and awoke in another, these disciples found that their original religion had completely changed.

The importance of this is to note that, according to the very close Companions of Muhammad (pbh) as found in many Tafsirs on the Quran, the strongly held belief was that a man who was a disciple of Jesus was actually crucified in Jesus' place. Note that the man is called a disciple and NOT one of the original Companions of Jesus.

There is an unknown historical source that states that Jesus at one point in time during his ministry separated himself from his Companions and crossed a river to hold a conversation with a man. The curious Companions of Jesus asked about this unusual behavior because Jesus told his Companions not to come with him. Jesus does not answer their queries directly. The man's name given in this unidentified source is Simon the Cyrenian. Of and by itself this means nothing but there is a paper trail of sorts to follow. This paper trail proves to be very interesting.

According to the New Testament, as Jesus was going to Jerusalem in his final 'days' Mark (10: 32) (4), he told his Companions the things that would happen to him in the future. Furthermore, John (13: 19) (5), and John 16: 16) (6), seem to show this. John (13: 19) is especially important as it declares that when things are done and finished that his Companions will have complete proof that he is who he said he was. Even though he discussed these things, it is well known that he spoke at times in parables (10) and it was not always easy to figure out exactly what he was driving at and this is discussed in the New Testament.

His Companions, who were not ignorant fools, did have faith in their prophet, did believe him to be the Messiah of sorts as direct witnesses to the many miracles that he performed, and had some basic grounding in the Old Testament. Besides this, they lived with him for nearly three years and saw him in deed and action. However, they were not completely tested and therefore their faith was not totally put to the test.

A new story emerges that may shock the Christians. One of Jesus' Companions who believed that Jesus was most definitely the Messiah had a little trick up his sleeve. He was not happy with the corrupt Jewish leadership and was very much against pagan Roman control of the Holy Land. He (being a so-called knower of the scriptures or at least in his mind he thought he was) knew that the Messiah would not be disgraced by his God. He also knew that the Messiah would be granted the power to take out the non-believer and kill the hypocrites. Unfortunately for this man, he also believed that waiting upon the Creator Lord's Will was too much a bother and if Allah had a Plan, then perhaps he (Judas Iscariot) could improve upon it. The arrogance of that man was too much and Satan deceived him by turning him into a traitor. Therefore, he contemptuously sold out Jesus for 30 pieces of silver hoping that by the grabbing of Jesus all heaven would break loose and that he of course would be the big hero along with the 'sleeping' Messiah. Instead of being patient and 'waiting upon the Lord', this man showed so much arrogance in his private council that Jesus had declared in the New Testament that it would have been better that he would not have been born.

So the soldiers came and grabbed Jesus but Jesus (pbh) had some amazing things to say and this is found in Math (26: 53-54) (7). Jesus declares that if he asks his Creator Lord for 12 legions of angels to come and defend him, they will come and no power on Earth could stop him or so we can surmise. However, the reason he does not do this is that he has complete confidence in his God and that he will submit himself to His Divine Plan completely and totally. Not only that, the previous scriptures have already declared his 'history' and he will be obedient to his God and His Will 100%.

The soldiers grab him as the scriptures of old say and they bring him before his accusers and these accusers are laying it on thick so that they could kill this imposter. They had determined to finish this 'devil' off because not only did he openly accuse them of being hypocrites but also because he declared other things like the end of their dominion as it would be given to another set of peoples. Finally, a discussion about Herod's temple that took 46 years to build took place, by which the liars claimed that Jesus was going to rebuild it in three days. According to the New Testament, Jesus claims that it will be his temple or body of which he spoke.

However, if Jesus said that it would be THAT temple (meaning a certain temple) instead of this (meaning his temple or body) of which they sought to destroy (kill), we have a completely different meaning altogether. The first meaning would suggest that he will die and resurrect his body. The second meaning is that he will resurrect another body—John (2: 19, 21-22) (8). Moreover, the Companions of Jesus did believe finally in all things especially when they understood that they would be more than totally humiliated and destroyed as to what occurred at the Real Last Supper. However, that last part deals with Quranic knowledge and will be given later as Allah Wills.

Before this Last Supper, the New Testament declares that some people, and false ones at that, asked for a SIGN. The New Testament in the Gospel of Matthew declares that only one sign will be given and that is the sign of Jonah—Math (12: 38-40) (9).

It does not make any sense that people would be gullible enough to believe any person coming around declaring himself the Messiah or anything else for that matter without bothering to see the evidence. In fact, the Gospel of John provides many examples of Jesus giving many signs of being the real Messiah. So how can we coordinate this apparent discrepancy? Well, there is no discrepancy at all!

In the Gospel of Matthew, Jesus was not speaking to believing Jews; he in fact was speaking with the Pharisees who were constantly baiting him as to his mission. Jesus could have given those disbelievers a thousand proofs and they would not have believed. Hence, the reply that Jesus gave them was the correct one. However, when it is understood that when people keep pestering their prophets OVER and OVER again about signs as Prophet Muhammad (pbh) declared, then it is understandable why Jesus calls these 'questioners' people that come from "an evil and adulterous generation."

Well according to the New Testament, Jesus was beaten very badly and hung on a tree or crucified in some manner and died a terrible death. Then after 3 days and nights, he became alive again. Before he suffered torture by the hands of his condemners and their sycophants, according to the Christians anyway, he went through a 'passion' of worry and asked his God to remove him from this 'death'.

However, even according to only the New Testament that action by Jesus makes no sense at all! I am not denying that Jesus' Passion took place! I am denying that for the reason they give, that it took place.

Jesus is a great man and a prophet. Not only that, but he holds a marvelous position as being the Messiah and one who is given a kingdom of blessedness upon his return. If other prophets and even non-prophets have faced death with absolute courage, trust and faith in their God and if some unbelievers have done the same, doesn't that appear to shame Jesus the son of Mary?

Even worse than this!!! When the New Testament readily declares that Jesus knew all of these things beforehand, as to what exactly was going to happen, and what was going to happen after that, it appears that it would make him a hypocrite to distrust his own prophecies, the prophecies about him in the Old Testament and it further shows a complete mistrust in his Creator Lord!

The picture provided in the New Testament shows Jesus as a man confident and completely ready to scold his close Companions for lack of true faith. Yet somehow, things seemingly are turned around and now Jesus seems to vacillate in a moment of weakness that we are supposed to believe happens to all men. However, that seems very improbable with a man of his stature and self-assurance.

Well according to Jesus in the New Testament, people would be able to see but not see at all. In other words, people would be able to see but not perceive what is happening—Math (13: 13) (10). After the crucifixion action took place, there had to be a physical body to take down from the cross, to administer to and to bury. So the Jews being well prepared and not to be taken advantage of by any form of trickery, were going to ensure that this imposter, villain and devil, who dared to accuse them of sitting in the false judgment seat of Moses, was going to stay buried—Math (27: 62-63) (11) Well, actually a physical body was put in a cave-like tomb and not thrown in a hole under the ground or left to rot on the cross.

A few days and nights after this monumental event (the non-crucifixion of Jesus), Jesus appears to his stunned and amazed followers as if he walks through a sealed room and causes quite a stir. After some disbelief on their part—Luke (24: 37) (12), they partake of a meal (the Real Last Supper) because this is no mere spirit but Jesus the Christ in the flesh who has something to prove to them as well as to show them. He is definitely not a spirit or a devil coming to taunt, ridicule or fool them. So he deals with the Old Testament prophecies and opens their understanding to his personal reality and their true positions—Luke (24: 44-45) (13), such that they may understand all things. And they proved to be completely faithful to their trust and feared not even under the pangs of death because of what they heard and what they finally realized to be the truth.

The Muslim Version of the Non-Crucifixion with Extra Comments

Mostly this part will feature the Muslim point of view of this event with slight variations depending on one's point of view. Surprisingly, Muslims can live with many of the suppositions put forth by the Christians as long as it is understood that Jesus was NOT put on the cross and he most definitely was NOT killed. However, a deep look into the possibilities of the non-crucifixion and its aftermath does help one to understand a few things about Allah and His Plan to a higher degree.

In fact, the Quran says a lot more about this event than most Muslims think that it does. It just does not seem possible that in only a few succinct verses, the Quran covers the whole story of what needs to be covered yet it does. If this turns out to be true, this is yet again another display of the awesome power of the Quran. Certainly, no amount of men, Jinns and Angels working alone or all together could ever come up with a Book like this!

The story of Jesus' turmoil is related in the Quran as to the unbelief he came across and how his Companions desired to be his helpers and faithful followers. That is not the real story we are about to embark on.

First, one should note that some human being was actually crucified. That human being was actually buried and was completely dead while being put inside the grave, or what is more accurate, the grotto. There was no switching of bodies or stealing of bodies. One completely dead man did go into the grave but only one very much healthy and vibrant man came out. Therefore, in a rather simplistic way one can say that someone 'rose' from the dead.

It is true that we cannot fully understand this statement especially when the original language may have carried with it certain meanings for the word 'dead'. As we shall find out a little bit later, the term death carries with it some subtle meanings, in particular to the word 'sleep'. Nevertheless, even here one is dealing with a sophisticated nuance such that one cannot be sure of a total explanation.

No religious person can claim to get everything in totality from the scriptures. For example, how long was the beard of Jesus or other such nonsense. But the important thing is to cover the essential parts of the story and get as clear a picture as to what we are allowed to get by Allah's permission. Not through mumbo-jumbo can we arrive at the understanding of truth but through diligence and understanding. So let us press on.

The understanding of the non-crucifixion of Jesus and what happened to him comes from only a few verses. The principle verses are as follows:

1. Q (S. 4: 157-158)
2. Q (S. 3: 55)
3. Q (S. 5: 112-115)
4. Q (S. 3: 48-49))
5. Q (S. 98: 6-7)

That in itself is quite amazing. After we take note of the following verses, then we should look at some historical evidence and use our common sense to see if it is possible to come up with the man who actually was crucified in place of Jesus of Nazareth (pbh).

After that, it might be a good idea to review just a few things the New Testament has to say about Prophet Muhammad (pbh). Some things may be quite new and not very well known even among Muslims themselves due to the lack of comparative religious studies.

The reason why the non-crucifixion was not a big, pressing issue for the Muslims is that it is <u>not essential for salvation</u>. It is true that the story and what surrounds it contains many valuable lessons but that story never rated what the Christians were to make of it. In fact, the historical evidence that we have to date about the making of the crucified Christ comes from around 148-150 AC. The formalizing of the Church of Rome was an ongoing process since the earliest part of the second century but became mostly solidified in around 140 AC as to Rome being the leading center of learning and trust.

In truth, the story of the crucifixion of Jesus had its adherents even before 80 AC but this was a matter for individual 'church' sects and even then it was not put down as being a certainty.

As was stated before, around 148 AC a man called Justin Martyr decided to end the bickering and in-house debates about whether Jesus was crucified or not. That should tell us something right there! Anyway, to settle the issue and what some of these awkward sayings found in a multitude of manuscripts from various church factions were saying (The original Greek New Testament guaranteed by church authority would not be formed until around 170 AC), Justin Martyr decided to get the 'real' truth about Jesus' crucifixion or non-crucifixion as the case may be by going to two sources: the Jews and the Romans. Therefore, the condemners of Jesus and the pagan Romans would decide the issue.

To the Jews, Jesus was considered an apostate and an imposter. Their records showed that he was put to death on the cross. The Romans who had no ax to grind against this man and who made a legend of keeping even minute records had also stated that Jesus was captured and crucified. Of course, one can understand why they said what they said. Even the believers witnessing the crucifixion saw with their very eyes the man called Jesus of Nazareth hanging on the cross. Later, many rejoiced at what really happened. The Jews could not for obvious reasons and the worldly Romans could care less for obvious reasons. Anyway, the dye was cast.

According to the best evidence presented to the world, the Islamic version of the non-crucifixion goes something like this. Jesus (pbh) asked one of his disciples to be a substitute for him on the cross. That disciple being filled with wisdom and true faith and inspiration by the Will of God chose to be the honored one and was given great status in the Hereafter. Common sense tells us, if we are honest with ourselves, that this discussion could <u>not</u> have been in the presence of Jesus' Companions otherwise they would have known all things. This can be verified by the close study of both the New Testament and the Quran.

Jesus (pbh) raised the dead with Allah's Permission only. Therefore, he raised the dead! Even though people may say that Lazarus was raised from the dead, which he was, this does not mean that Jesus had his hands tied and could not raise anyone else.

Now, when one looks at certain verses in the Quran, one may be lulled into primitive thinking that Allah is making but a simple list of things Jesus did. It is as if this is a mere 'grocery list' of sorts and forms no connection with history. How absolutely absurd and disrespectful of the Quran that is!!! We are looking at the miracle of Jesus with Allah's Permission of taking a lump of clay and forming it into a bird and breathing into it and it becomes a living creature! Q (S. 3: 48-49) (14). Yes, he did do that and a bird flew away.

However, there is a lifeless decaying and beaten up body in that grave (grotto) that is laying there as a lifeless lump of clay. It was a battered body ripped in flesh by whipping, with a broken nose and terrible wounds of crucifixion. There was also the spear wound, which ended that life as blood gushed out. In other words, it, as scientists know very well, was a body under decay or **corruption** as the Biblical phrase would put it.

It is a scientific fact that immediately after death occurs the body will start to decay instantly although it won't be physically noticed for awhile. However, Biblical prophecy says that Jesus or what is more accurate, the Messiah's body, will not see corruption at all. This could be taken to mean that he was not killed or simply put that he did not die.

After several days and nights, a body left that grave (as the grave could not hold that man). However, the body that left that grave was a glorious one of perfect flesh and soul. It was not a weakened body as all wounds were healed! Do we have proof of this and can we be nearly certain whose dead and mutilated body WENT INTO THE GRAVE AND WHOSE BODY ACTUALLY CAME OUT OF THE GRAVE! YES WE HAVE THAT KNOWLEDGE WHEN CORRECTLY APPLIED. First of all, it must be repeated quite strongly, although the unbelievers may detest it, that JESUS, IN TRUTH, WAS NEVER PUT ON THE CROSS AND HE NEVER DIED BUT WAS RAISED UP TO THE HEAVENS IN BOTH THE PHYSICAL BODY AND WITH HIS SOUL!!!

If that seems like an impossible task, then one has underestimated the power of the Quran. Let us now look at the Quran with some depth and find that logical thread that with Allah's Permission can open the doors to what happened in the events that have mystified many Christians for so long.

In these verses Q (S. 4: 157-158) (15), it is declared that Jesus was not killed or crucified but was raised up to his Lord. That is true. However, the Quran has some surprises for us. Another verse Q (S. 3: 55), (27) states that Allah says ("I will Take You)—meaning 'put Jesus to sleep'. Being put to sleep is not the average run-of-the-mill snoring type of sleep. What kind of sleep was it? If we are not told precisely what kind of sleep it was by Arabic understanding, then it would be just guesswork. Suffice it to say that it was some type of <u>special sleep</u> because a body was regenerated.

Now as to Jesus moving around <u>without detection</u>, the answer is very simple. In the New Testament Jesus was surrounded by his enemies who went to grab stones to kill him and he simply vanished. The same happened with Prophet Muhammad (pbh).

The Prophet and 'Umar were sitting together and along came the wife of Abu Lahab. She approached 'Umar with fire in her eyes and spittle from her mouth desiring to get at the Prophet, scream at him in her hatred, and even rip into his face. 'Umar who could have told her to take a walk sat there dumbfounded. Why could she not see the object of her sulfuric hate? When she left, the dumbfounded 'Umar asked his Prophet about this. Muhammad (pbh) told him that an angel came down to him and covered him with his wing. So what is so mysterious about Jesus (pbh) undergoing the same condition? That we have proof of in the New Testament as he avoided the angry crowds several times during his ministry.

As to the body or temple, Jesus declared what he was going to do if those hypocrites went to destroy the temple of the body. And we do know that he was given the power to raise and heal the dead with Allah's Permission. So what is strange in that?

The real telltale signs are still to come!!! One of the most important group of verses in the Quran about this issue comes from Q (S. 5: 112-115) (16). It is amazing what these verses have to say and they do say a lot.

Most people are under the notion that the Last Supper of Jesus and his Companions happened just before the crucifixion episode. It has come down to us from what seemingly is in the New Testament to the modern idea generated in a painting by Leonardo da Vinci. ARE THESE IDEAS WRONG? If they are, then probably they put people off on the wrong track.

The concept of the Last Supper is indeed a festival to celebrate and Christians around the world do celebrate this festival in their remembrance of the Passover Meal. However, is that the REAL Last Supper? It appears with the aid of Quranic understanding that that supper was not the Last Supper at all.

The story given in the Quran is but a few verses long yet it contains an awesome power of information and when compared with what the New Testament only partially alludes to, gives the believer a real insight concerning Jesus the son of Mary (pbh) and his Companions.

Polycarp, an early church father, did express his displeasure about the Roman Church changing the date of this festival with the result that it seems there are now two festivals instead of one. This, of course, of and by itself, proves nothing as it is an isolated incidence but isolated incidences can add up. Let us now look at what can be called the holy festival or Solemn Festival that supersedes any Passover Meal. According to the Quran:

Behold! the Disciples said: "O Jesus the son of Mary! Can your Lord send down to us a Table set (with viands) from heaven?" Said Jesus: "Fear Allah, if ye have faith"

They said, "We only wish to eat thereof and satisfy our hearts, and to know that you have indeed told us the truth; and that we ourselves may be witnesses to the miracle."

Said Jesus the son of Mary, "O Allah our Lord! Send us from heaven a Table set (with viands), that there may be for us—for the first and the last of us—a Solemn Festival and a Sign from You; and provide for our sustenance, for You are the best Sustainer (of our needs)."

Allah said, "I will send it down unto you; but if any of you AFTER THAT resists faith, I will punish him with a CHASTISEMENT such as I HAVE NOT INFLICTED ON ANY ONE AMONG ALL THE PEOPLES." Q (S. 5: 112-115)

The Passover Meal or the supposed Last Supper is where Jesus and his Companions were sitting around a table and eating food. Then the traitor Judas does his ungodly thing and Jesus eventually is turned over to a squadron of Roman soldiers. After that, certain interrogations, beatings, torture and a crucifixion follows. However, Jesus, before he was taken into custody, had told his Companions to go and await him in a certain 'safe' house for a few days and nights. So far, there is no problem in this. Jesus, after the so-called crucifixion event, is going to do what he said he was going to do and we do know that he was given the power to raise the dead.

Anyway, his Companions are not just shut in a room but they have what can be considered 'spies' or friends/helpers (defined here as members of the same sect of believers) who report on the extremely important events taking place. After all, Jesus had a large following and the fact that their Messiah is taken prisoner and facing a big tribunal is not just boring news. It turns out to be a very big deal. Because it is not a ho-hum event but an extremely pivotal one, it is a natural that the trial of Jesus and the events that followed would be closely monitored throughout.

However, we are led to believe from falsified history that the Companions were without resources and that the swelling numbers that were attracted to Jesus were all a bunch of simpletons and cowardly to boot. That just does not make any sense at all!

These friends of the Companions do report to the safe house concerning the events happening to Jesus. He has been sentenced and that what their own eyes saw was a tortured, tormented man hanging on a cross until he expired. These friends of the Companions are trustworthy and would not lie about such a thing.

Many people believe that it was easy for God the Creator Lord to fashion the universe in all of its complexity. However, some people will baulk at the idea that God could find it easy to make an exact duplicate of the body of Jesus right down to the mole on his back. In other words, a complete 100% exact replica down to the very number of electrons contained in that body. It is no wonder that people saw Jesus on the cross! How could people think otherwise?

The story continues in that after a few days the Companions of Jesus were getting extremely restless and afraid (12). After all, let the truth be known. If they (the enemy) grabbed and killed what they thought was the trouble making imposter, what are they going to do with his 'faithful' Companions who might be tempted to carry out his faith? They certainly will go after them also. So, we can see what is actually now taking place. The Companions of Jesus are in a deep mood of anxiety and are in quite a danger of losing their faith.

In the midst of their consternation and inner-squabbles into a sealed room walks Jesus and, according to the New Testament and the Quran by interpretation, they are not overjoyed. In fact, they are fearful and very much put out. Yes, it is great to have Jesus there with them but how could he get into the room? Not only that, he is supposed to be dead, and if not, maybe he is a ghost or spirit come to say that his preaching was good but he just didn't cut it as the Messiah.

The Companions were not ignorant men. They did spend about three years in his presence learning about real faith and seeing him do wondrous things. However, they were taught that even the Satan could appear as an angel of light as is stated in the New Testament. Although they did not know that Satan could appear in any human form except that of Prophet Muhammad (pbh), they still were very cautious and feared lest they become of those who were duped as happened in the past with other historic Messianic movements.

An interesting story of one caught in a deep mood of anxiety concerns 'Umar. He was the second righteous Caliph in Islam and one of the fortunate people who were promised Paradise. In the Quran, the Prophet himself was warned about the consequences to himself if he were to follow the lusts of the disbelievers. What then of 'Umar if he were to commit a heinous act? After hearing that his beloved Prophet (pbh) had died, which at first he refused to believe, he threatened anyone who would mention such a possibility by death with the sword. Spilling innocent blood of another Muslim for no just cause is like killing the whole nation. The penalty for that is Hell-Fire. However, thanks to timely action 'Umar was prevented from carrying out his threat. The purpose here is to show that even men of great strength of character can, when under terrible strain, act with abnormal behavior or illogically, even for only a brief period.

Study the Quranic verses mentioned previously as they show a strained group of Companions who nearly fell into disbelief. It is OK to ask for a settling of their hearts but the impudence of those people appeared when they asked Jesus if he was telling the truth! Imagine, after all those years of being intimate with him, seeing his miracles and listening to his directions, they had the gall to ask for proof positive that he was not Satan. They implied that when they wanted a Sign to show them that in fact he was telling the truth and not a liar.

The important thing lies in the very terrible warning given to them by God. If after that event or miracle of the Table of viands, they did not have 100% perfect faith, they would be punished worse than any of the people ever had been punished before. That is saying a whole lot and gives us further clues as to when this event took place.

The New Testament does give some details about this holy of holy festivals but it is rather on the light side and not with what one would expect. It does not even mention the Table of viands at all. It does discuss somewhat the fear of the Companions and that Jesus renews the faith with them through scriptural explanations of the mysteries of the faith (8), (13). In reality, this most holy of festivals marks the point where the true teachings of Jesus would eventually lead to a scripture called the New Testament being produced, and the faith being eventually spread to millions of people. Hence, the importance of this very, Solemn Festival cannot be overstated—as it is in the current New Testament.

A Good Seed Gone Bad—The Story of Basilides

Muslims know that Allah is the turner of the hearts and He can turn them in any direction He likes.

The historical reality of the man called Basilides has been lost through the ages but what can be pieced together is quite revealing. Once again, one finds the paper trail of this affair continuing. Through warnings given in the current New Testament, it appears that Basilides is nothing more than a little anti-christ—1 John (2: 18-19) (17) 1 John (4: 1-3) (18), 2 John (1: 7) (19), and Acts (20: 29-30) (20). He, in fact, is very much similar to the man called Abdullah ibn Saba in Islamic history as to the havoc he raised among the 'flock of believers'. His philosophy of false Gnosticism blended in with Christianity caused the teachings of the real faith of Jesus no end of trouble. In fact, from the epistles of John to Acts one finds warnings about certain people who will come forth like wolves in sheep's clothing who were members of the faithful but who left the faith to turn into devils spreading mischief throughout the land.

What we do know about this man is that he at one time was a member in good standing of one of the varied 'churches'. That he was well enough advanced in knowledge and studies of the teachings of Jesus to hear from a disciple of Peter, a man called Glaucias, that Jesus was not crucified but that a man called Simon the Cyrenian was actually crucified in his place. We know that Basilides was well advanced in Christian literature because he actually wrote about twenty-four pieces of literature concerning the Gospels as well as other so-called Christian writings.

Well Glaucias died and Basilides could do as he pleased and what we know about his system of gods and their sons and his comment on the Old Testament and his belief system based on two unknown so-called prophets provides a big key to his foolish philosophy. He even has Jesus being pure spirit and without a corporal body such that he can explain with silliness how he was not crucified!

It is important to remember, however, that people like Basilides or Abdullah ibn Saba (Abdullah the Jew as he is sometimes called) do not wear a sign on their chests screaming out 'I am an abject liar'! They come in like wolves in sheep's clothing by stealth and try to deceive the vain and foolish by clever tricks. This is how they spin their poisonous webs of deceit by catching the unwary and the foolish, who have defective hearts, in a tangled mass of deception. In fact, let it be known that these evil people start by declaring the truth as they build up their aura of confidence and then slowly sow seeds of dissension.

Sometimes, however, one can gain something from a heap of garbage as is known from the famous hadith (concerning the Ayat Al-Kursi) showing an encounter between Abu Hurairah and a Jinn. The end result was as the Prophet (pbh) declared, "The LIAR has told the TRUTH." Well, in that case, the lying Jinn did tell the truth but one has to be very careful in all cases. Suffice it to say, there is some accreditation to the idea that it actually was the man called Simon the Cyrenian who was crucified in place of Jesus.

A fast reading of the current Gospel according to Luke might leave one puzzled as to who was crucified. Of course, the man who was carrying the cross went up the hill and was crucified. According to Luke's Gospel, the man carrying the cross was not Jesus but Simon the Cyrenian.

A deep study into history reveals some peculiar oddities about that man. As far as anyone knows, he was a very important piece of history to early Christians as being The Man who was face to face with the Master on that fateful day. It is even stated that his two sons later became followers of the Way of the teachings of Jesus. As to the fate of Simon the Cyrenian, he drops out of history as if he had vanished from the face of the Earth, never to be seen again.

At various times throughout history, certain philosophies have sprung up to explain the non-crucifixion idea. One of the chief contenders for the 'man' on the cross has been Judas Iscariot the traitor. That is a laughable notion because the Jews would have loved to see a squirming, whining person being confused and begging for his life. The Romans would have recorded this ungodly scene and that just did not happen.

Another idea put forth by certain Christian sects is that Jesus was a <u>pure spirit</u> and therefore could not have suffered a real death by crucifixion. This notion goes against all of the revealed scriptures of the People of the Book because Jesus (pbh) was a man who had to eat his 'daily food' or else he would have died. As far as being a spirit in form that would <u>not</u> have been a credit to him, because he is set forth as a <u>human example</u> and the call of 'come follow me' would ring hollow as well as being superfluous.

Another thought held by certain sects of various religions is that Jesus was on the cross but somehow recovered from his 'mortal wounds' to live for awhile before he died and then was buried secretly somewhere so his 'sect' could carry on and spread the message. This also is against revealed religious thought. Others have claimed that he survived his ordeal and went into hiding and then left his religious followers for a well-earned vacation in India where he finally died. That is total nonsense!

Finally, some misguided individuals believe that the Quran is not straightforward and unambiguous but talks of his 'surviving' as what might be called as surviving only in the minds of his followers and in God's memory but that he died a physical death. That also is utter rubbish.

All of these suppositions have no basis in fact and rip away at the fabric of Divine Revelation. The Christians started the importance of the matter of crucifixion versus non-crucifixion as they developed their theories as to the relationship between God and man and the necessity of a 'go-between' because man is essentially a bum and can never rise to the occasion of going directly to his Creator Lord. Therefore, God is essentially out of reach and seemingly needs an intermediary to settle His affairs.

This is completely erroneous when all the revealed scriptures are studied. In fact, it is slanderous to suggest that the One and Only God has needs or wants anything. Moreover, it suggests that His system is so imperfect that in order to fix a defect in His Plan He had to have 'help'. It is man that needs help and that is true but under the system set forth which is through the one brotherhood of prophets and Guidance as to what they brought and not through magic or some quick fix. The idea of the one brotherhood of prophets allows man to think more clearly concerning the notion of all the sons of Adam and not a racial, tribal, sectarian philosophy.

Recently there has been a movement underway to show that the Quran is not complete nor is it to be considered a real Holy Book due to its being compiled in a haphazard way with missing verses in its various chapters (Suras). This laughable attempt at mimicking the knowledge of the incomplete reliability of the Old and New Testaments is foolhardy but it shows what some people will do to cause doubt among the minds of the faithful.

To counteract such nonsense is to ask for the evidence to be presented outright. Indeed! The evidence can be presented outright but what kind of evidence is presented? Is it from mainstream Islam? The answer is no. What invariably is found is that certain rejected hadiths, forged hadiths and various people who for lack of a decent word were of the hypocrites and acknowledged as such by mainstream Islam at the time are given great weight and precedence even when it is clear that these people are nothing but magnanimous liars.

No person in his or her right mind would take a little anti-christ like Basilides, pretend he was a real Christian due to his so-called Christian writings, then go on to take his corrupt philosophy, and proclaim it as the real message of Jesus the Christ!

Clever criminals (devils) have a tendency to 'blend' in some truth to their corruption so that they will not be taken by all and sundry as insane. Therefore, their game is easy to spot in some ways as these liars try to alter the truths by weaving them in a web full of deceits. It is always important to investigate such sources and let those who have the knowledge point out where such information is coming from and who is peddling such information and why are they peddling such information and in what manner are they peddling such information.

People have a right to their own opinions and if one believes that the world is flat, so that is what the person believes. However, sowing seeds of mischief and willfully lying against the Word of the Creator Lord is punishable by the Hell-Fire as is explained in His Word.

The Passion of Christ

The Passion of Jesus is one of the most critical points of the whole story of the supposed crucifixion. People could ask, "Why is it that if Jesus knew that he was not going to be crucified, that is, he knew about the future events to happen in his life, should he undergo such a trial of passion?" In other words, the Passion of Jesus becomes a grasping straw for those who would choose to believe that he was actually crucified.

It has been said that a drowning man will grasp at any straw that will save him, or in this case, save his concepts. Well the Passion of Jesus was an internal affair within side himself as the New Testament so admirably puts it. He has reached the pinnacle of success and his apparent reward from all of his struggles that he put forth for the sake of God in doing His Will is to undergo humiliation heaped on top of humiliation by a thankless lot of humanity. This is not a way to celebrate or honor the 'great liberator'.

Caging a vicegerent like a zoo animal to be abused and tormented is not something to look forward to even from this high level man of great distinction. And who could blame him? One might expect Jesus (pbh) to take a nonchalant attitude if he was so much in the know. However, a human being is a human being after all and no human being in his elevated position would relish the treatment that he was about to receive. Although he received this humiliation willingly, which is not difficult to understand because as he said before, 'But how then should the scriptures <u>be fulfilled</u> that thus it must be' (7). And he, being truly flesh and blood and not spirit in form, did feel that pain and humiliation that he might fulfill prophecy without opening his mouth. And those who did put him in that situation did represent the world as to its aversion to the truth in which they must answer and in which they were deluded. They decided that they as masters of the universe would overrule the One God and would not become deluded but in the end their plots and plans turned against them and those who would deceive became those who were deceived.

To further understand something of the Messiah-soul in reference to this matter, go to the next chapter, *A case of shock and awe # 1.* In this chapter there is an Old Testament verse that discusses the Messiah and this verse was set down nearly 700 years before the start of Jesus' mission as the last of the Jewish prophets. This verse delivers an understanding of the excellence of the Messiah for those who understand.

How does one deal with this subject? Well, the Old Testament does mention in several places including the Psalms and Isaiah, to name a few that the Messiah will suffer. The New Testament declares that Jesus must suffer and die but that by itself contradicts the New Testament, which declares that it is given to man to die once, Hebrews (9:27) or as the Quran so nobly puts it, as man will die when his term of appointment becomes due. And because Jesus must return (very much alive) then a belief in his death before he comes back is very strange not to mention very, very wrong!

Perhaps the best way of looking at the Passion of Christ is in looking at the passion of 'Uthman the third righteous Caliph in Islam and one of the great successful men of faith who, as a member of an elite group, was guaranteed Paradise. How do you think this holy man should be treated? Would it be proper and righteous to spit in his face and to heap garbage on his head? That would be unheard of but that is what happened to him!

Can you imagine that the high office of being Caliph with great armies under one's command will be put under a period of 'humiliation' by a force of 200 people and then a mere 2,000 people? The story of the 'siege' in the holy city of Medina is one that brings sorrow and tears.

'Uthman's face turned very red upon hearing a secret from his beloved Prophet. He knew because of the experience on Mount Uhud that one day he would be martyred and of course, he knew that something would happen during his life that would rip the very fabric of his beloved Islam through contentions and Fitna. However, he must be strong to resist the temptations of spilling Muslim blood and going against the Divine Decree. Yes, it was in his power to call the various mighty armies to silence the hot heads (who believed but were reckless) and the hypocrites who hid behind a cloak of so-called fairness but he chose another route.

And he actually won the day as his words of compassion and gentleness seemed to quell the horrible rebellion. However, Satan does not rest and will not be defeated so easily. So some 'Judas' thought to expedite matters by forging letters aimed at the various groups who had made Fitna their meal.

The Caliph had sworn an oath to Allah to pardon the rebels and to overlook their foolishness. But certain letters appeared with the private seal of the Caliph set on them to let the detractors go in peace until they reached a certain distance and then have them all slaughtered to the last man. The hot heads and hypocrites returned to Medina, and after a fashion, butchered the Caliph and waves upon waves of Fitna (civil strife) came upon the body of believers throughout the intervening years.

As for the Passion of Christ what is wrong in that? Here is a man mightier in the eyes of Allah than any Caliph. Here is a vicegerent, a holy prophet and the man who must return to lead a paradise on Earth from whence all will believe in him before he dies and the world will be changed to holiness. In other words, here is the Messiah of the Age who can call on many legions of angels to defend him. Yet according to prophecy mentioned above, he did not defend himself but underwent the ordeal of being tormented and tortured without whining or opening his mouth to defend himself!

Of course, he knew that he wasn't going to be crucified! However, being such a high and elevated man in the eyes of God does take a lot of ENDURANCE and WILL POWER to follow His Commands and bow down to His Will. Even the Prophet (pbh) when he was horribly mistreated and bleeding from the arrogant ones from the city of Taif, refused to let the Angel destroy them by rooting up a mountain and smashing them to pieces. So, what is wrong with the Passion of Christ? It is that he must 'SUFFER' as the scriptures of old say but he, in truth, did not die nor was he even put on the cross!!!

CONCLUSION

As in all my writings, of which there are some things that are hard to understand, the message has been clear. There is only ONE God, One Messiah and One chosen Way. All Praise, Honor and Glory belong to Him for without Him nothing would be made that is made and He is the One Who is without needs or wants for He is the Real Reality and none can compare unto Him!

I have no doubts that Jesus (pbh) rose from the dead but it is better and clearer to say that he had the power given to him from the One God to raise the dead. Because it appears that no 'normal' man could do this, many have been overcome by confusion. It is in the power of a true vicegerent to do this when it is so decreed by the Creator Lord.

Some people have grave doubts that a beaten-up body like the replica of the body of Jesus could miraculously be healed. However, the Quran states (14) that Jesus could heal the sick and wounded so it would be easy to heal himself. Besides this, the New Testament declares by itself that the healer (physician) (25), (26), should first heal himself before healing others lest he become in danger of being a hypocrite and Jesus the son of Mary (pbh) was no hypocrite.

Whether the debate is about rising from the dead in that he rose from the world of unbelief (22), or that he actually caused the dead body in his likeness to become alive or that both are the case, does not affect the pathway of true belief one iota. One is not called by the prophets to forego common sense, the following of the pathway of true values (Sunnah) and the worship reserved for only ONE God.

The story of the non-crucifixion of Jesus (pbh) can be understood from one of the New Testament's verses that contain a prophecy of what will take place in 'church' history in the future and a saying from Prophet Muhammad (pbh). According to the Prophet (pbh) (in paraphrased form) the true Sunnah of their prophet (Jesus) would be taken away (caused to be forgotten) proportionally according to their actions of their getting away from the essentials of their faith. Moreover, according to the leading Companion after Jesus arose to the heavens (Peter), there would be men whose wits would be defective and whose basic knowledge of the continuity of the scriptures would be defective and they would create massive damage to the truth by misrepresenting the truth and polluting it with their invented corruptions (24).

In my second book, *Kill the Beast*, the non-crucifixion was touched upon lightly and a discussion of one hadith about Jesus and what he will do on his return was mentioned. Here is an excerpt from that book pages 5-7.

"This book, *Kill the Beast* shows a few beasts that are real. Most of the beasts that man has to deal with are systems or ways of life that are somehow a poor copy or a mimic of the way things should be in reality. Since mankind is connected to each other by a spiritual creation in that at one time we were all one nation, systems have sprung forth from the collective psyche to mimic that which is from above. One of the simplest ways to explain this is to declare it the guidance of the prophets versus the copycat version of real life. Some systems are better than others as to their depth or ideals but no system that is made on Earth can equal the perfection, which has been sent down from above.

An example of this comes from what Jesus (pbh) will do when he returns to Earth. An Islamic hadith declares that he will <u>break crosses and kill swine</u>. Let us assume that this will be interpreted only literally. Some enterprising, young devil may want to decide he could keep Jesus hopping around day and night for decades by simply starting a massive campaign to produce billions of crosses and ship them to all countries and territories thus making Jesus a very busy man. Not only is he going around breaking crosses, he is also butchering pigs and wild boars even in the deepest jungles of whatever country. No doubt there is some literal interpretation (to be found in this hadith) but to believe in the above interpretation is mind-boggling to say the least.

However, a deep understanding of the full records gives us another picture. The foundation of the Messiah and what was promised him as to his kingdom by the Creator Lord was laid down in the previous book. This then forms the basis of understanding that breaking crosses is the dissolution of all systems not in accord with the Way and that the killing of swine is the perishing of the hypocrites. For if even one system were allowed to remain intact, his victory would remain incomplete and would be a reminder of a mockery set before his blessed face.

When it is declared in the New Testament that a sword will come from his mouth, or in hadith literature when it is mentioned that blood will be shown on his spear or that he will be able to defeat evil by his breath as far as he can see, the killing of swine seems to take on a more understandable meaning.

In preparation for his coming, why can't we as a collective whole change the order of things, trot out a better understanding, say a few prayers, go our merry often inconsiderate ways and postpone or get rid of the notion that billions of people will die in a relatively short period of time? Because the Creator Lord had a plan and He will keep it. Neither His Plan nor His Wisdom can be questioned. As for us, it is not given in this age anyway that an ant can stop a runaway train. Breaking systems by coming to a collective consciousness is way above our current means and may even cause more hardship. Besides, not everyone is on the same page as it were in soul development so the idea of a radical life change instituted by man to come into the conformity with the truth is not practical. It is the individual and his/her responsibility and awareness that are important. Growth by leaps and bounds is not only impractical but also unhealthy.

Should we be perfect? Some people say that we should because Jesus is reported to have said to be perfect as your Father in heaven is perfect. However, life is built on steps and stages and not by leaps and bounds. I am sure that if Jesus said that statement that he meant others to try and fathom the complexities of life in relationship to the spiritual laws."

In retrospect, it is up to the believing peoples to understand these matters as best as they can and to take them in the Proper Perspective—from original prophetic channels. If the crucifixion idea is important to the individual, then that is what must be. However, true faith is not dependent on one single event but in what is in the secret chambers of men's hearts.

The end result does not come from the desires of men because the truth does not depend upon man's faulty and often superfluous desires. No one can get beyond their station and the truth belongs with the One God Alone.

What man can fathom of the so-called crucifixion event is that while one real dead man was put in a grave (grotto), only one man came out but he came out not with a broken nose, cruelly placed whip marks, bloody wrists and pierced ankles or even a mortal wound in his side. In fact, what came forth from that grave was a complete and whole body that was not bleeding nor did it have a mark on it like some gory sideshow freak. It was a miracle that took place but a miracle that cannot be fully fathomed by men. However, we are not left in the dark to wander around in circles but are told the basic truth and must rejoice in this pure truth that Jesus the son of Mary was not put on the cross to be crucified nor was he killed but so it was made to appear unto those who saw that event. And those who argue about the case (opposing) Allah's Pure Word are left to be in doubt and confusion with nothing but conjecture to follow.

And we are warned especially in the Quran to be upright in our thinking and not to chase after the Unseen which cannot be known by any man. We are told to believe in the One God, the God of all of the creation and to have faith in His Divine Plan and to leave that which cannot be known alone.

And pursue not that of which you have no knowledge; for surely the hearing, the sight, the heart all of those shall be questioned (concerning this). Q (17: 36)

Narrated An-Numan bin Bashir: I heard Allah's Messenger (pbh) saying, "Both legal and illegal things are evident but in between them there are doubtful (unclear) things, and most of the people have no knowledge about them. So whoever saves himself from these unclear things, he saves his religion and his honor. And whoever indulges in these unclear things is like a shepherd who grazes (his animals) near the Hima (private pasture) of someone else, and at any moment he is liable to get in it. (O people!) Beware! Every king has a Hima and the Hima of Allah on the earth is His illegal (forbidden) things. Beware! There is a piece of flesh in the body if it becomes good (reformed), the whole body becomes good, but if it gets spoilt, the whole body gets spoilt and that is the heart." (Bukhari)

Who receives guidance, receives it for his own benefit: who goes astray does so to his own loss: No bearer of burdens can bear the burden of another. Q (17: 15)

But the people of their own accord cut asunder their (one) Creed into many religions yet they will have to return to Us. Q (21:93)

When it is said to them, "Follow what Allah (God) has revealed" they say, "No! We shall follow the ways (and practices) of our ancestors." What! Even though their fathers were devoid of wisdom and guidance." Q (2: 70)

When Jesus came with clear signs, he said: "Now have I come to you with Wisdom, and in order to make clear to you some of the (points) on which you dispute: therefore fear Allah and obey me."

For Allah, He is my Lord and your Lord: so worship Him: this is the straight way."

But sects from among themselves fell into disagreement: then woe to the wrongdoers, from the Chastisement of a Grievous Day! Q (43: 63-65)

Let not the unbelievers think that Our respite to them is good for themselves: We grant them respite that they

may grow in their iniquity: But they will have a shameful punishment. Q (3: 178)

Compare this verse with the New Testament's verses found in 2 Thessalonians (10-12):

And with all deceivableness of unrighteousness in them that perish; because they received not the love of the truth, that they might be saved.

And for this cause God shall send them strong delusion, that they should believe a lie:

That they all might be damned who believed not the truth, but had pleasure in unrighteousness.

People were called to take Revelation seriously and apply those 'constraints' to their worldly affairs. Even though we have not overcome the world (23), and become a vicegerent right blessed, we are still tested for our veracity of faith and our intentions. Therefore, we are measured as to what is in the secret chambers of our hearts and we pray to Him Who is the Only One to answer prayers, that we may be guided to His Light and seek out His Forgiveness, Grace and Mercy. Amen!

Verses Discussed in This Chapter

1. And verily it (the Quran) is announced in the Scriptures of former people. Q (26: 196)

2. For then will I turn to the people a pure language that they may all call upon the name of the Lord, to serve him with one consent.
   From beyond the rivers of Ethiopia, my suppliants, even the daughter of my dispersed, shall bring My offering. Zephaniah (3: 9-10)

From the New American Standard Bible we get:

For then I will give to the peoples purified lips, that all of them may call on the name of the Lord, to serve Him shoulder to shoulder.

From beyond the rivers of Ethiopia My worshipers, My dispersed ones, will bring My offerings. Zephaniah (3: 9-10)

3. Or do you think that most of them understand? They are only like cattle—nay, they are even farther astray from the Path. Q (Sura 25: 44)

4. And they were in the way going up to Jerusalem; and Jesus went before them: and they were amazed; and they followed, they were afraid. And he took again the twelve, and began to tell them what things should happen to him. Mark (10: 32)

5. Now I tell you before it come, that, when it is come to pass, you may believe that I am he. John (13: 19)

6. A little while, and you shall not see me: and again, a little while, and you shall see me, because I go to the Father. John (16: 16)

7. Do you think that I cannot now pray to my Father, and He shall presently give me more than twelve legions of angels?
   But how then shall the scriptures be fulfilled, that thus it must be? Math (26: 53-54)

8. Jesus answered and said unto them, "Destroy this temple, and in three days I will raise it up.

Then said the Jews, "Forty and six years was this temple in building, and will you rear it up in three days?"
But he spoke of the temple of his body.
When therefore he was risen from the dead, his disciples remembered that he had said this to them; and they believed the scripture, and the word which Jesus had said. John (2: 19-22)

9. Then certain of the scribes and of the Pharisees answered, saying, "Master, we would see a sign from you.
But he answered and said to them, "an evil and adulterous generation seeks after a sign; and there shall no sign be given to it, but the sign of the prophet Jonas.
For as Jonas was three days and three nights in the whale's belly; so shall the son of man be three days and three nights in the heart of the earth." Math (12: 38-40)

10. Therefore speak I to them in parables: because they seeing see not; and hearing they hear not, neither do they understand. Math (13: 13)

11. Now the next day, that followed the day of preparation, the chief priests and Pharisees came together unto Pilate.
Saying, "Sir, we remember that the deceiver said, while he was yet alive, <u>after three days I will rise again</u>."
Math (27: 62-63)

12. But they were <u>terrified and afraid</u>, and supposed that they had seen a <u>spirit</u>.
Luke (24: 37)

13. And he said to them, “These are the words which I spoke to you, while I was yet with you, that all things must be fulfilled, which were written in the Law of Moses, and in the prophets, and in the Psalms, concerning me.
    Then opened he their understanding, that they might understand the scriptures.
    Luke (24: 44-45)

14. And Allah will teach him the Book and Wisdom, the Torah and the Gospel.
    And (appoint him) a messenger to the Children of Israel, (with this message): “I have come to you, with a Sign from your Lord, in that I make for you out of clay as it were, the figure of a bird, and breathe into it, and it becomes a bird by Allah’s leave: and I heal those born blind, and the lepers, and I bring the dead into life by Allah’s leave; and I declare to you what you eat, and what you store in your houses. Surely therein is a Sign for you if you did believe.” Q (S. 3: 48-49)

15. That they said (in boast), “We killed Christ Jesus the son of Mary, the messenger of Allah”—but they killed him not, nor crucified him. Only a likeness of that was shown to them. And those who differ therein are full of doubts, with no (certain) knowledge but only conjecture to follow, for of a surety they killed him not.
    Nay, Allah raised him up unto Himself; and Allah is Exalted in Power the Wise. Q (S. 4: 157-158)

16. Behold! the Disciples said: “O Jesus the son of Mary! Can your Lord send down to us a Table set (with

viands) from heaven?" Said Jesus, "Fear Allah, if ye have faith"
They said, "We only wish to eat thereof and satisfy our hearts, and to know that you have indeed told us the truth; and that we ourselves may be witnesses to the miracle."
Said Jesus the son of Mary, "O Allah our Lord! Send us from heaven a Table set (with viands), that there may be for us—for the first and the last of us—a Solemn Festival and a Sign from You; and provide for our sustenance, for You are the best Sustainer (of our needs)."
Allah said, "I will send it down unto you; but if any of you AFTER THAT resists faith, I will punish him with a CHASTISEMENT such as I HAVE NOT INFLICTED ON ANY ONE AMONG ALL THE PEOPLES." Q (S. 5: 112-115)

17. Little children, it is the last time: and as you have heard that an anti-christ shall come, even now are there many anti-christs; whereby we know that it is the last time.
They went out from us, but they were not of us; for if they had been of us, they would no doubt have continued with us: but they went out, that they might be made manifest that they were not all of us. 1 John (2: 18-19)

18. Beloved, believe not every spirit, but try the spirits whether they are of God: because many false prophets are gone out into the world.
Hereby know you the Spirit of God: Every spirit that confesses that Jesus Christ is come in the flesh {is a man} is of God:

And every spirit that confesses not that Jesus Christ is come in the flesh is not of God: and this is that spirit of anti-christ, whereof you have heard that it should come; and even now already is it in the world. 1 John (4: 1-3)

19. For many deceivers are entered into the world, who confess not that Jesus Christ is come in the flesh. This is a deceiver and an anti-christ. 2 John (1: 7)

20. For I know this, that after my departing shall grievous wolves enter in among you, not sparing the flock. Also of your own selves shall men arise, speaking perverse things, to draw away disciples after them. Acts (20: 29-30)

21. Those who disbelieve, among the People of the Book and among the Polytheists, will be in the Hell-fire, to dwell therein (for aye). They are the WORST OF CREATURES.
Those who have faith and do righteous deeds, THEY ARE THE BEST OF CREATURES. Q (S. 98: 6-7)

22. But Jesus said to him, "Follow me; and let the dead bury their dead." Math (8: 22)

23. These things I have spoken to you, that in me ye might have peace. In the world you shall have tribulation: but be of good cheer, I have overcome the world. John (16: 33)

24. And account that the long-suffering of our lord is salvation; even as our beloved brother Paul also

> according to the wisdom given unto him has written to you.
> As also in all his epistles, speaking in them of these things; in which are some things hard to be understood, which they that are unlearned and unstable wrest, as they do also the other scriptures, unto their own destruction.
> You therefore, beloved, seeing you know these things before; beware lest you also, being led away with the error of the wicked, fall from your own steadfastness.
> 2 Peter (3: 15-17).

In my other books, I discussed at no mean length some of the sayings by Paul that were indeed difficult to understand if not taken in their proper context. There is no need to beat a dead horse to death nor is there a need to lock the barn door after the horses have bolted.

Paul, being one of those rare Gnostic types, said things that could never be appreciated without a true context put around his words. There are also grave doubts as to the credibility of some of his statements as this was not from him but from people who enlarged and clarified his works. There are even some suggestions that others came along and put in their own two-cents worth as they tried to make things clear about things they had no understanding of whatsoever.

An example of this is an early church father by the name of Polycarp who was far removed from Paul by several decades and was a simple character. That is no denigration on Polycarp but how could he possibly understand Paul who was miles above him in understanding and who actually met some of the original Apostles and had discourses with them? The danger of falling prey to the impure of heart came during Paul's era and beyond and caused much dissension amongst the true believers that would eventually lead to confusion and much infighting. This itself can be gleaned from New Testament writings that give ample warnings to those who were fighting to keep the faith and teachings of Jesus (pbh) intact.

Therefore, for those who would suggest that I have ignored the wondrous Paul concerning the crucifixion matter are much mistaken and are directed to my other books where these things are more than amply documented. In truth, Paul did not believe that Jesus was put on the cross but that after 3 days, Jesus did come out of the grave or as he puts it 'arose from the dead'. As to a measure of Paul's credibility, one can turn to **appendix A** featuring the *Acts of the Apostles* and **appendix B** for a background on Paul.

25. And he began to say to them, "This day is this scripture fulfilled in your ears.
    And all bare him witness, and wondered at the gracious words which proceeded out of his mouth. And they said, "Is this not Joseph's son?"
    And he said to them, "You will surely say to me this proverb", 'Physician, heal thy self: whatsoever we have heard done in Capernaum, do also here in your country'.
    Luke (4: 21-23)

26. And why behold you the mote that is in your brother's eye, but consider not the beam that is in your own eye?
    Or how will you say to your brother, "Let me pull out the mote out of your eye; and, behold, and a beam is in your own eye?
    You hypocrite, first cast out the beam out of your own eye; then shall you see clearly to cast out the mote out of your brother's eye. Math (7: 3-5)

The above quote has several meanings but as it is stated in the New Testament, Jesus spoke in many parables so that the unwary would not perceive or understand. Therefore, his statement of 'they see but do not see and they hear but they do not understand' is as true today as it was in his time.

27. And (remember) when Allah said: "O Jesus! I will take you and raise you to Myself and clear you of the blasphemies of those who disbelieve … Q (S. 3: 55)

According to the Tafsir of Ibn Kathir, the words 'take you' refer to a form of sleep and according to the Quran sleep is a form of death—(6: 60) and (39: 42). It is not profitable to go beyond this point except to mention that the raising up idea, being totally correct, does not imply a time factor such that one second, one hour, day or week should be attributed as to when Jesus was raised.

It is He Who takes your soul by night (when you are asleep) and has knowledge of all that you have done by day, then He raises (wakes) you up again that a term appointed be fulfilled, then (in the end) unto Him will be your return. Then He will inform you of that which you used to do. Q (6: 60)

It is Allah Who takes away the souls at the time of their death, as well as those that do not die during their sleep. He keeps those (souls) for which He has ordained death and sends the rest {back} for a term appointed. Verily, in this are signs for a people who think deeply. Q (39: 42)

It is an article of faith in the belief that Jesus was raised up to Allah. However, it is not an article of faith to know the time of his raising. According to the historical document that also strongly declares the coming of Prophet Muhammad (pbh),

Jesus stayed on Earth for 40 days after his 'Passion'. Note that it does not declare after his crucifixion but after his passion.

To whom also he showed himself alive after his passion by many infallible proofs, being seen of them forty days and speaking of the things pertaining to the kingdom of God. Acts (1: 3)

It is important to note that this most instructive author, that is, the author of *The Acts of the Apostles* mentions the Passion of Jesus in this verse but does not mention the supposed crucifixion. This is not a serious error on his part. People who really care to dwell on the truth of the matter with great care in their thinking and those who have knowledge will see that the Passion of Jesus and the supposed crucifixion came one after the other.

So what does this really imply? The statement made by this unknown author implies that the most important event about these times; the most memorable event about these times would be the Passion of Jesus and not the crucifixion. In other words, the idea of the crucifixion was not in his mind considered of the utmost importance and did not compare with the Passion of Jesus. One cannot know this for sure but it is only logical that this is the correct interpretation and history tends to bear this out along with the Quran and hadith material.

The history of the EVOLUTION of the Christ being crucified has been discussed in brief from before in this book. That history shows that even when **some** of the church sects accepted the crucifixion of Jesus at an early date of around 80-85 AC, it took a long time for the cross and the legend of the cross to bear its fruit of prime importance. If the early Companions and the true second generation of believers were not outspoken about this 'mystery', then a comparison of these true saints to the later day 'fools' will cause the primary followers to look stupid and the later day philosophers to look like geniuses. However, such is not the case and the supposed crucifixion idea of Jesus being crucified is in the end result pure unadulterated fiction!

According to the above thinking, Jesus (pbh) was finally resurrected in body and soul after 40 days thereby completing his job on Earth until he is recalled to enter the Earth again at his second coming. In other words, his mission for his first coming is now completed. Therefore, the mystery of what can be known is known and what can't be known is unknown. Moreover, it is not an article of faith to guess the particulars that would not add to our faith though it is helpful to clarify the articles that strengthen the faith. Thus, clarity in religion is always positive and hopefully the One Who made all things for He is the Dominate, the Wise will accept this piece!

MUHAMMAD IN THE BIBLE—NEW TESTAMENT

There are so many places that the Prophet of Islam is mentioned in the Bible, both the New and Old Testament, but sign after sign given to a disbelieving folk will not accomplish anything. Still, there are some intriguing mentions of the Prophet (pbh) that some may not be aware of and that coordinates well with Islamic Science.

Does the New Testament actually threaten about the dire consequences in disbelieving in the Oneness of God and His Chosen Messenger? Yes, it does and these statements must be looked at with great care and consideration. Here are some quotes taken from the current New Testament. This also provides further proof that the current New Testament can lead someone to Islam but Scriptures must be studied with reverence and not be used as a toy or plaything!

The following few verses talk about the new Prophet to be given and the return of Jesus or his Second Coming. It should be remembered that these declarations concern mostly the return of the Promised one whereby he will lead the world into a united faith under the banner of pure Islam. Those who would oppose this or who have hypocrisy in their hearts will be destroyed.

And He shall send Jesus Christ {the second coming}, which before was preached unto you:

Whom the heaven must receive until the times of restitution of all things, which God has spoken by the mouth of all his holy prophets since the world began.

For Moses truly said unto the fathers, " A PROPHET SHALL THE LORD YOUR GOD RAISE UP UNTO YOU OF YOUR BRETHEREN, LIKE UNTO ME; HIM SHALL YOU HEAR IN ALL THINGS WHATSOEVER HE SHALL SAY UNTO YOU.

AND IT SHALL COME TO PASS, THAT EVERY SOUL, WHICH WILL NOT HEAR THAT PROPHET, SHALL BE DESTROYED FROM AMONG THE PEOPLE. Acts (3: 20-23) See Appendix A concerning the words 'your brethren'.

This quote is further substantiated by certain Gospel verses such as the following:

The son of man shall send forth his angels, and they shall gather out of his kingdom all things that offend, and them which do iniquity;

And shall cast them into a furnace of fire: there shall be wailing and gnashing of teeth. Math (13: 41-42)

The importance of Muhammad as to the WAY as to the chosen Faith and a comparison to the very short Quranic Sura AL-Kauthar is shown in the following New Testament verses.

However, note the name of the Holy Ghost being substituted here.

Wherefore I say to you, "All manner of sin and blasphemy shall be forgiven unto men: but the blasphemy against the Holy Ghost shall not be forgiven unto men.

And whosoever speaks a word against the Holy Ghost, it shall not be forgiven him, neither in this world, and neither in the world to come." Math (12: 31-32)

To clear up this issue of whether the Holy Spirit or Gabriel is discussed <u>or a man</u> is talked about; these verses put it in a more clear sense:

In the last day, that great day of the feast, Jesus stood and cried, saying, "If any man thirst, let him come unto me, and drink.

He that believes on me, as the scripture has said, out of his <u>belly shall flow rivers of living water</u>."

(But this spoke he of the Spirit, which they that believe on him should receive: for the Holy Ghost was not yet given; because that Jesus was not yet glorified.)

Many of the people therefore, when they heard this saying, said, "Of a truth this is <u>The Prophet</u>.

Others said, "This is the Christ." But some said, "Shall Christ come out of Galilee?" John (7: 37-41)

There is a hadith that says that on the many occasions that Muhammad (pbh) was fasting, a sound of what could be called a <u>bubbling noise</u> as likened unto a pot when its boiling could be heard from his belly. So there it is.

What seems to be a problem with these verses—John (7: 37-41)? The basic problem is the lack of understanding comparative religion and history. How is it so?

First of all, these verses seem to be allegorical and there seems to be no true way of understanding them. That complaint is only partially correct. The second problem seems to be that the wording used is not concrete enough for an understanding and also the imagery of the wording seems bizarre. Finally, verse number 39 "But this spoke he of the Spirit …" seems just a little too convenient to be from the original penned work.

The problem can be solved through an understanding of comparative religion and history. Before that happens, imagine a literal concept of these verses. Is there a spirit whose body will open up and cause to gush forth a river like the Mississippi River from his abdomen? That idea does not make any sense at all.

What does make sense is the idea generated from the Dead Sea Scrolls about the spirit of truth being a cleansing spirit. In other words, all false conceptions on religious issues will be thrown down and truth will be brought forth. Water is looked at in many cultures as symbolizing cleaning or washing away the dirt, or in this case, falsehoods that have mired the religious scene.

What about the belly part? Granted that is a little bit strange but historically a man can be measured by his 'guts'. In addition, the strength of an army can be seen from the saying, 'an army travels on its stomach'. Also, a man's quality or even a nation's quality can be measured by the so-called bread basket which for a man would be his abdomen.

Recent history concerning Biblical understanding has shown that when going back to the most original, complete New Testament documents, several verses once considered part of the New Testament have been purged from the new, revised form of the New Testament. Why is this so? This is so because Biblical scholars have found that a few verses contained in older versions of the New Testament were the result of some long ago critic penciling in, on the outside margins, his own thoughts. Later on, these penciled in thoughts which were not a part of the original document were made to appear as original verses by being incorporated into the original.

Verse number 39 from John (7: 37-41) appears to be a blatant forgery in the sense that it is an addition inserted to make it appear to coordinate with another gospel discussing the time of glorification of the Christ. However, this glorification in John appears to be different from that gospel's version in that it is concerned with Jesus' conquering the grave (non-death) and being judged as a true vicegerent scenario found in John's Gospel (16: 14). Anyway, the unknown author of verse 39 seemingly wants to harmonize this saying found in John with another Synoptic Gospel talking about something different and he doesn't give any indication of understanding these verses at all!

When certain verses are put under the strictest of scrutiny for the purpose of understanding, certain concepts and ideas are brought to light. Hopefully, the God of all the sons of Adam will accept this understanding brought forth.

Verily, We have granted you (O Muhammad) AL-Kauthar. Therefore, turn in prayer to your Lord and sacrifice (to Him only). For he who hates you shall be cut off from all future hope. Q (Sura 108)

What can a man or woman do if he/she wants to hear from Jesus as to what to do? Simply follow his advice of going to the spirit of truth (That Prophet):

And when he is come, he will reprove the world of sin, and of righteousness, and of judgment:

Of sin, because they believe not on me;

Of righteousness, because I go to my Father, and you see me no more;

Of judgment, because the prince of this world is judged.

I have yet many things to say to you, but you cannot bear them now.

Howbeit when he, the Spirit of truth, is come, he will guide you into all truth: for he shall not speak of himself; but whatsoever he shall hear, that shall he speak: and he will show you things to come.

He shall glorify me; for he shall receive of mine, and shall show it unto you.

John (16: 8-14)

Some people argue over the change in the Greek words for the 'Comforter' (Paracletus vs. Periclytos). It is better to go to the original language, which has been proven as the speech of the 'common man' of the day whom Jesus came to, and that language is Syriac. This language was the major language in Palestine for over 100 years even after it became a Muslim nation! The word Jesus used for this 'spirit of truth', and he did not speak Greek, was Munhamanna the Syriac word.

Who was Jesus? A look at the Quran Sura 98 verses 6 and 7 tell us what we need to know (21). Jesus was a man. He was not half man or half Jinn or half angel. According to Abu Hurairah's interpretation of these verses, man is the highest of the creation being likened to a vicegerent given great dignity and power. That would be so given the fact that man originally was higher than the angels. So, what does this imply? It would imply that as Jesus was raised up and cleared of the blasphemy that was heaped on him; he now is in a great position of dignity and power but still only a man—a man as he was meant to be and not a lowly creation. And as a vicegerent right blessed, he will return on the Day he is told to come forth leading mankind into true faith in a kingdom right blessed. A kingdom united under the banner of truth, righteousness, and justice. Truly, this kingdom will be a paradise on Earth as men and women will worship with harmony under the banner of Islam.

As to the debate of whether Jesus (pbh) has undergone a partial judgment or has been judged, that is, cleared from all falsehood that was charged against him, the verse in the Gospel of John (8: 11) claims that he has been judged. It does not claim that he will not be a bystander on the Last Day of Judgment because he will as will all the prophets. The important thing about this verse is that Jesus as the 'prince' of this world has been judged and therefore according to that judgment he is entitled to be a Vicegerent. Moreover, in understanding the term Vicegerent, one gets to understand a glimmering of the position of power he is raised up to.

A CASE OF SHOCK AND AWE # 1

A surprising verse written in the Old Testament around 700 years before the start of the mission of Jesus the son of Mary (pbh) discusses the Messiah-soul and his beginnings. This is the verse from the Revised Standard Version of the Bible:

But you, O Bethlehem Ephrathah, who are little to be among the clans of Judah, from you shall come forth for Me one who is to be ruler in Israel, <u>whose origin is from of old, from ancient days</u>. Micah (5: 2)

This one little verse says it all. Maybe to some it will be a surprise in that all three world religions agree in the soundness of this verse but perhaps not the meaning. Just because Judaism, Christianity and Islam agree perfectly that this verse has meaning does not mean that everyone sees things the same way or that one should believe things in the same way.

This important verse needs only to be discussed in a fundamental, foundational way because that is the best way and that is the strongest way. In this method, things become clearer and more fruitful. Furthermore, it is noteworthy to notice that since the religions agree, the religious differences that occur will come from the people and not from the One God. Therefore, it is safe to assume that the troublemakers and corrupt individuals are those who reject harmony and truth, look for huge differences as in 'my god is better than your god' and finally prove they do not know what they are talking about. Empty barrels do make the most noise as well as being practically useless.

A basic breakdown of this key verse shows some amazing things that should have all of the Abrahamic religions celebrating the cause of truth and justice. But since that won't be a universal happening, it appears that religion will still be held hostage to the determent of those willing to gamble their own souls for the sake of a miserable though finite gain.

From Bethlehem Ephrathah which is a small town near Jerusalem on the West Bank of the Jordon River, regarded by many as an early home of David (pbh), and the place where Jesus is said to have been born shall come forth a servant of the Most High, standing up for the One God, who shall rule ISRAEL and his beginnings started from times of old—in ancient times.

One has to remember that this verse representing the Word of God is nearly 700 years older than Jesus so it is a prophecy about some person who will be exalted and given rule over ISRAEL. Furthermore, his beginnings, because he has a beginning, is from some time in the past but before this past, he was not. This person is specially chosen by the One God and obviously, he could not choose himself.

The problem arises when one uses a type of one-dimensional thinking. It is completely true that Jesus the son of Mary never occupied a place of being ruler over ISRAEL but that leads one on the quest of defining ISRAEL. It is clear from the above verse that a prophet will come from Bethlehem who will become the Messiah and he will rule over the servants of God.

The above verse can be proven from many pathways and it is only the contenders and rebellious people who have darkness in their hearts who will not believe it.

First, the only recognizable person fitting this description of place of birth was Jesus the son of Mary. It is true, as was said before, that he did not rule over Israel. Of course this is logically so because his job, according to the scriptures, is not finished but he shall return to rule ISRAEL as prophesied in the New Testament, Quran and hadith material.

But the term 'ISRAEL' is in dispute. That is not the case for those who understand. ISRAEL is not a land or a country but translated according to the correct reading of the scriptures means, "those who are the true servants of Allah (God)" such that the kingdom promised to the Messiah is the whole world and All the peoples living on that world from north, south, east and west. This point is also attested to in the New Testament, Quran and hadith materials.

This unified kingdom of believers will be united in one faith (One Way), sharing one ideal and living in harmony without strife, jealousy, greed or hatred. And all who are alive at that time of his glorious reign will believe on him and those who do not or who have crookedness in their hearts will be destroyed from amongst the peoples such that none will be left whose open or deeply hidden desires would run counter to this Messiah.

This is also found in the New Testament, Quran and hadith materials.

Most of these 'proofs' have been written down in my previous books as well as some being presented in this book.

Unfortunately, some people consider the God to be their private pet as if they can manipulate Him as a storefront dummy is manipulated by one changing its clothing. Down through the ages, different peoples have claimed that God favors them according to birthright, religion, race or creedal beliefs. That notion is repugnant and strictly prohibited in all of the scriptures.

There is no such thing as God's chosen people as to being a particular race. However, there is an expression or idea of such a chosen people but this definition, which is not contrary to religious thought, concerns those who have followed the WAYS OF GOD via the teachings of His Messengers down through the ages. This means that anyone who adheres to the pathway of his prophet (at the time of that prophet) belongs to that set of peoples called faithful or the chosen ones. That by definition covers a lot of prophets and a lot of peoples.

From this universal understanding comes the spiritual understanding that ISRAEL is not a state set up by the hands of men, but a condition defined as the true servants of Allah (God) and this concerns the membership of those people in being taken as 'chosen'.

The headstone for this resurgence of the blessed kingdom to be, for there must be a physical place, is in the land of Palestine most notably in the city of the holy priest of old (Melchiziedek) and is called Jerusalem. And this mighty soul from of old has been mentioned in some of the scriptures with some significance.

Islam does not reject these things but further adds to the understanding of these ideas. In honor of the Messenger Muhammad (pbh) that Eternal Way shown by the One God is called Islam and the followers of Islam (the Way) in any age are called Muslims. The term Muslim is not synonymous with the term Arab or any Semitic peoples as most Muslims today are not Arabs or Semites.

However, the reemergence of the true knowledge of faith started with a group of people known as Arabs, the revered Book in Islam called the Quran is originally in Arabic, and the Prophet himself was an Arab born in the land of Arabia. This was not by his choice but by God's Will and therefore the Quranic Arabic Language is revered and kept as the medium that ushered in the 'clean' knowledge of the Divine.

In accordance with the position of Jesus and Muhammad as to Jesus being the activity and Muhammad being the Messenger of the Messengers, one finds the expression of faith as one who expresses That Faith. In other words, one (Jesus) leads by that faith (Islam) in his second coming. A hint of this is said to be found in Isaiah as the one who rides the donkey is speaking with the one who is riding the camel.

A second feature from the verse found in Micah 5: 2 is the fact that this great Messiah has a beginning. The beginning is from ancient times but we do not have to fret about that because it is clear that the meaning says that the Messiah-soul, Jesus the son of Mary (pbh) had an origin. Therefore, as great as the Messiah is, he does have an origin. To suggest that God had a beginning is not only repugnant but also criminally evil. The One True God has no beginning and no end and is expressed simply and beautifully in the Quran like this:

> **Say: "He is Allah, the One; Allah, the Eternal, the Absolute; He begets not, nor is He begotten; and there is none like unto Him."** Q (S. 112: 1-4).

Therefore, the concept of the Messiah—Jesus the son of Mary—is that of a man raised to a high level but a man like any man or to put it succinctly, a common, ordinary man who is a member of the human race. Being a member of the human race means that he is not more human or less human than any other human but his distinction comes from the quality of being obedient to his Lord and being gifted by his Lord and reaching the potential of man in the scheme of creation by his Lord. Hence, his origin (creation) didn't come from his power or plan but he, like a normal soul, had to be guided, protected and empowered all the days of his life by his God, the God of all men.

Another interesting point that can be taken from Micah (5: 2) is the theory presented by this author for the actions of Judas Iscariot. Why did he turn in his beloved leader?

Obviously, the Messiah according to all the Holy Scriptures is going to be a very powerful source and an individual that no person would want to contend with (after the Gog and Magog are dispatched). But that is on his return, 'second coming', not on his first mission. Therefore, if one mistakes this issue and tries to subvert prophecy, that person will end up going astray due to his delusions no matter what his or her so-called good intentions were. As is often said, "The pathway to Hell is paved with good intentions." Therefore, the one who knows the right approach is way far above the one who is ignorant. Thus, one finds the downfall of Judas Iscariot.

And it was Jesus and his close Companions who should have been listened to for they were the ones that laid out the directions for the coming of That Prophet—Prophet Muhammad (pbh).

A further interesting point that can be developed from this scripture is the concept that all Major Prophets are foretold in advance of their coming. This can be a really important point when trying to ferret out the real prophets from the anti-christ imposters. Specifically speaking, there have been no prophets between Jesus (pbh) and Muhammad (pbh) and Muhammad (pbh) is the last of the line of prophets. There have been contenders but where and how were they foretold? Their followers no doubt can bring but only ambiguous verses, if any, into the fray. And these verses would be so ambiguous as to be totally useless.

What is the offshoot of all of this? The same for Jesus as for Muhammad and that is in the expression of the word 'sign'. Many signs were given to the people of Jesus' reality and this idea can be found in the Quran and the Gospel of John.

When taking his audience into consideration (the treacherous Pharisees) and in knowing that they had received many signs from before, it is easy to see the insult heaped upon them by the tongue of Jesus. After giving many signs to these people, he gets angry at their incredulous ignorance and diabolical plotting in showing a lack of any true faith and declares that only one sign will be given to them. But to who? He clarifies this when he proclaimed to these pretenders of faith that they were an evil and adulterous generation.

Because they persisted in abuse and irreverence to the truth, they were punished and sent strong delusions such that to them Jesus was no more than a heretic and a fool. Yet they were made fools because they trusted their senses and believed they had killed Jesus (pbh) whom they hated above the love for the truth. And Jesus being like everyman but of such a high standard of character, the disbelievers actually were deceived thus making it true that they, the would be deceivers, would become deceived as is reported in the scriptures.

A CASE OF SHOCK AND AWE # 2

One of the most beautiful events found in the Quran is summed up in verses 90-92 of Sura Yunus (Jonah). It concerns the story of Pharaoh's death. These verses seem simple and clear enough and indeed, they are. Scientifically/psychologically speaking, it is an awesome event for those who perceive.

We took the Children of Israel across the sea, and Pharaoh with his hosts followed them in oppression and hatred, till when drowning overtook him, he said, "I believe that none has the right to be worshipped but Allah in whom the Children of Israel believe, <u>and I am one of the Muslims</u> (those who are believers by submitting their wills to Allah)."

Now (you believe) while before this you were an unbeliever and you were one of the (evildoers and corrupters).

So this day We shall deliver your (dead) body (out from the sea) that you may be a sign to those who come after you! And verily, many of mankind are heedless of Our Signs.
Q (10: 90-92)

Scientists at times are on record as to investigating certain strange phenomena occurring in the lives of man. One such phenomenon is that what might occur to the human in a near-death experience. According to investigative reports concerning near-death experiences, some individuals experience a rare phenomenon whereby within a few seconds of 'real' time the would be victim of impending death gets a chance to go through his or her life experiences as if that person were watching something akin to a movie.

Of course as we would understand it, that seems impossible to fit a near lifetime into a few seconds. Therefore, since scientists do not really know much about the brain and its capabilities or even about the phenomenon of space/time itself, they are left puzzled by these rare occurrences. All that they could say if these experiences are true is that time, as we know it, would seem to behave different under different circumstances much like water behaves differently in its different states—liquid, vapor and solid.

The Pharaoh of the above Quranic verses was an abnormally cruel individual especially to the followers of the One God. In fact, he considered himself a god. Moses (pbh) who was a member of the human species like Pharaoh (both recognized this) took divergent pathways and in part this competitive ideology was to find one who would succeed and one who would be a loser. The loser was Pharaoh although at times it looked completely different in worldly terms, because Pharaoh seemingly held all the cards.

When Pharaoh was confronted with many wondrous miracles (the blue-plate special of wonders and Signs) he seemed to give the appearance of believing in them but not in the right way. Because of his arrogance and egotistical pride, Pharaoh seemed to believe that Moses (pbh) was tapping into some magical source of which he would like to get his hands on.

Pharaoh is a common, ordinary man but under very uncommon circumstances and he is about to become a Sign unto mankind though he did not of course know it at the time. He is getting to see directly the blue-plate special of 'shock and awe' instead of theological debates and so he is going through phases drawing him ever closer to his doom. Even though he is being setup for the slaughter, he conforms to humanity in general in that he is given chance upon chance upon chance to repent yet he still stands arrogant and ignorant of the Reality and that what awaits him. Pharaoh does truly believe in the afterlife. However, his concept of the afterlife was as corrupt and twisted as his soul.

Pharaoh seems to be a real Sign unto people who do not take heed. A Sign of the opportunities given but thrown away and a Sign of Judgment to come based on past actions and not the final awakening of truth.

We now see Pharaoh in his final days in a corrupt rage against Moses and the people of Moses. Pharaoh, stripped of his dignity by his own actions, reverts towards his natural self for he cannot break the bonds of destiny when his god-like position that he so loved and coveted overcame the purpose of his creation:

And I (Allah) created not the jinn and mankind except that they should worship Me (Alone). Q (51: 56)

Now he will pursue Moses and his followers and utterly destroy them and put to rights his own godhead and kingdom of greatness. He is about to embark on one of the greatest adventures of his tragic life—an appointment by which his soul will be shown Reality—The Reality of which only a few have been shown before.

As the sea parts and divides into twelve channels for the twelve tribes to go forth to safety on the other side of the land, Pharaoh leads his massive army in hot pursuit. The enemy of God, the God of Moses, is closing in on the stranded group of faithful that has crossed over to the other side when lo! The massive walls of water towering like mountains and held back from collapse to allow Moses (pbh) and his people to cross in safety start to rush down upon Pharaoh and his legions.

It is now only seconds from sure death as the mountains of water come cascading down in a rush and a furry. But to Pharaoh, the onrushing water which will destroy him and his massive army is now moving in his eyes only at the pace of a walking ant while to the others its momentum is swift and furious and is closing in for the kill.

Pharaoh's soul is now in the grips of another time, another reality. His soul is stripped of its fetters and it sees clearly now with eyes that do not lie and truth that does not hide. He has entered into a new dimension—a dimension of awareness far above earthly concerns. This is a dimension where Reality is separated from amusement and play on Earth:

Know that the life of this world is only play and amusement, pomp and mutual boasting among you, and rivalry in respect of wealth and children. (It is) as the likeness of vegetation after rain, thereof the growth is pleasing to the tiller; afterwards it dries up and you see it turning yellow; then it becomes straw. But in the Hereafter (there is) a severe

torment (for the disbelievers—evil doers), and (there is) Forgiveness from Allah and (His) Good Pleasure (for the believers—good doers). And the life of this world is only a deceiving enjoyment. Q (57: 20)

The soul of Pharaoh knows his creation and knows the truth about his Creator even though he cannot see Him. With the dust from his eyes cleared and freedom from all distraction erased, he now submits to the truth for no lies or deceptions can stand between him and the Throne of the Lord of all the worlds. Because there is only One Way, he submits to that Way as would only be natural and begs to be written down as a Believer in earnest:

"I believe that none has the right to be worshiped but Allah in whom the Children of Israel believe, and I am one of the Muslims (those who follow the truth in any age)."

However, his game has played out. He does not command here in the presence of the Throne. Seeing Reality will do his soul no good. Just like those of the corrupt nations before him who were destroyed and saw in their souls before death overtook them in their state of worldly preferred insolence, Pharaoh's soul is castigated and outright rejected as being of the worst of creation and fit only for the lowest depths of Hell-Fire. A fitting reward for what his soul willfully coveted above common sense even when given chance after chance to awaken from disbelief.

Now the terrible and mighty waves that only seemed to approach by centimeters at a time resume their real time motion because, in truth, these waves never would be seen by mortal eyes to go so slow and they came crashing down with their full intent to kill.

All of these things happened in a matter of only a few seconds of earthly time. Pharaoh, whose arrogance allowed him to dodge all the signs and wonders given to Moses (pbh), did express real sincerity and repentance and showed perfect understanding and desire to be a true servant of the One God. But there is a limit for all things and it was too late for him and his realization meant absolutely nothing. Why? Well, for many reasons it was too late. A look into the many hadiths discussing the Last Day of Judgment gives us knowledge that the souls of humanity will not be in a debating mood to challenge the Reality appearing before them when the time comes.

All that they can do, if handed their records in their left hand, is to blame others (Jinn and men) for misleading them from the pathway of truth and cursing those 'others' whom they stupidly followed. In other words, their railing cry is not against the unfairness of the Creator Lord but against others as well as their own selves for being contemptible. And when they pray for Mercy, their prayers in acknowledging the Most Merciful are fruitless because He won't acknowledge them—a fitting reward for what they reveled in and were want to do.

Because their secret records will be finally opened, they will see that, like Pharaoh, they were given many opportunities to repent but chose to claim Allah's Mercy and Wisdom was repugnant to them. Unlike Pharaoh, in a way, we do not know about these ample opportunities and only the foolish or the liars claim to be knowledgeable about these hidden things. Unlike Pharaoh, we are not given blue-plate special miracles to experience directly so our deaths are not so noteworthy or traumatic nor are we singled out to be a special 'Sign' for the peoples.

And this is not a one-time occurrence because it happened to the criminal nations in the past when as nations they were destroyed except for those who believed and were allowed to escape. And this is not over as a famous hadith declares concerning the time just prior to the entrance of Jesus the son of Mary (pbh). After the sun will set in its place of rising, a person who then makes a sincere proclamation of faith or who has not gained anything by his faith but does deeds of merit, it will not be accepted from him just as Pharaoh's sincere proclamation was rejected. The universe and its set laws are run by Allah's Will and not by the flimflam, lame and pathetic excuses from tin-horn gods who trampled around the Earth as if they were of any real importance.

Abu Hurairah reported God's Messenger as saying, "The last hour will not come before... earthquakes are abundant, the time becomes short, dissensions appear and there is much harj, which means slaughter, ... before a man passes another's grave and expresses the desire that he were in his place, and before the sun rises in its place of setting. Then when it rises and people see it they will all believe, but that is a time when a soul will not be benefited by faith it did not have before, or acquire any good from its faith." (Bukhari and Muslim)

So when they saw Our punishment they said, "We believe in Allah Alone and reject (all) that we used to associate with Him as (His) partners.

Then their faith could not avail them when they saw Our punishment. This has been the Way of Allah in dealing with His slaves. And there the disbelievers lost utterly (when Our torment covered them). Q (40: 84-85)

A CASE OF SHOCK AND AWE # 3

The truth about the Gospel of John is not totally clear. Most Christian scholars are in agreement that this gospel was initiated between 90-100 AC but a few hold out for a date as early as the 60s or even as late as the 130s AC. Surprisingly, most relevant experts in the field believe the author of this gospel to be an unknown non-eyewitness to the events of Jesus. That would be strange indeed!

The problem with this gospel is that it appears that two different hands wrote it but that a third hand revised it while bringing it into an acceptable format of 'current' beliefs. In truth, it appears that most of this gospel was written by one person before 90 AC and retouched by a close companion of the first author in trying to protect its existence. So, we have a virtual agreement as to its truth in a large part of its verses considering that the original writer was the beloved Apostle,

John son of Zebedee and the second author appears to have been his disciple who also was named John.

Critical scholarship has found several 'holes' in this gospel to shed doubt on its purity. It does seem that only a few decades past before the Gospel of John underwent the knife of a clever surgeon. Whether the third compiler was a man called Cerinthus or not, it seems that chapters 19 through 21 have been skillfully changed. The notion of the real Last Supper seems out of sync with even the Synoptic Gospels and of course there is the so-called crucifixion issue which seems to read well but in truth is really botched up.

The vast majority of the Gospel of John is probably true but that doesn't make it understandable as to who Jesus really was. Even those of good faith but weak in scripture might become confused. So who is this Islamic Messiah or the noblest of souls? He is a common, ordinary man who earned the right by God's Will and by His Will alone to be that Sign to mankind. All power is given to him because he is a man who succeeded and came into his inheritance. Therefore, all power deserving to be held by a man called a Vicegerent (as some men are) is given to him because of God's Promise to the sons of Adam.

This Promise dictates that a person, any person, who succeeds in a certain type of judgment, has the right to be amongst the company of the highest of created beings including the Angels. As for Jesus (pbh) he declared it of himself but giving all due respect to his Creator and knowing full well that he could do nothing of and by himself save for His Creator's Will.

How do we know this for sure? We can know this because before the so-called crucifixion scenario he spoke truthfully that:

…"I have overcome the world." John (16: 33) and "Of judgment, because <u>the prince of this world is judged</u>." John (16: 11).

If he passed judgment of a certain kind as the Quran says Q (S 3: 55) then he should inherit a dominion promised to him. And as he arose to the heavens as a vicegerent, he shall return in the fullness of power given to him as Vicegerent. He must fulfill his duties in giving honor to his Lord and must commit (bow down) to His Plan and reign in power and dignity in Islam and then die because he is a man and as a man he must await the Last Day of Judgment as all men are constrained to do. However, he will not be standing with others but will stand with his own kind—the one brotherhood of prophets as witnesses for or against those who are to be judged.

This honorable prince of the world is not King but a prince serving his KING—the Only KING—Allah (God).

The Gospel of John poses a major difficulty for the Peoples of the Book. The difficulty is in recognizing what kind of gospel it really is. Historically, the early church had a big problem with this gospel and argued about it over the years as to its authenticity. This gospel began to gain acceptance as a 'true' gospel between 110-115 AC. It must be remembered, however, that different sects of Christians had different 'readings' so the Gospel of John was not universally accepted as a major work by all of the faithful. That plus the possible various authors lending a hand to this gospel was also responsible for its lack of historical backing.

However that may be, the Gospel of John is quite different from the other three Synoptic Gospels because it was written in a certain style, at least originally, and this style has caused a tremendous amount of pain for many people.

Like it or not, this gospel appears to have been written by one of the rarest of individuals called a real Gnostic. Unlike the cheap imitations floating around after the time of Jesus, and there were many, this writer at times dwells on the status of the Messiah. He does not hide the excellence of the Messiah but proclaims it. However, under no situation does this author proclaim that Jesus was any more than a man and a righteous servant of the One True God.

Other people might disagree with this assessment but the original author of this gospel knew very well that another prophet was to come and WHY he was to come and he didn't hide that fact either.

The real problems with the Gospel of John are several Gnostic sayings which if not taken in context with the other records, chiefly the Old Testament, will cause havoc with the church even before 100 AC. And when one looks at the original writer as John the beloved Apostle of Jesus and follows his surviving letters in the New Testament, one can see that he delivers a strong warning to those who will try to make mischief with the truth.

In fact, Paul, another real Gnostic and a rarity of the times because 99 out of 100 of them seem to be liars, describes the whole process in a nutshell. He talks about **Divine Destiny** and that no one will be able to overcome it. In fact, he is giving a very strong warning that the vile mischief-makers have practiced deceit somehow or have deceit in their hearts and that the One God will deceive them and cause them to slay themselves (their souls) such that their own destruction will be by their own perverted hands.

A strong statement to make but one that is reinforced by the Quran as that it is what the hands of man have passed on from before that has become their undoing and that it isn't the One God Who is responsible for their choices but that they chose themselves to walk down the road of self-destruction even though they were given many chances to enter the Light. They, through their arrogance, simply refused to follow common sense and treated the one brotherhood of prophets as perverse trouble makers.

Where does Paul declare this? He declares this in 2 Thessalonians (2: 3-12):

Let no man deceive you by any means: for that day shall not come, except there come a falling away first and that man of sin be revealed, the son of perdition {the Anti-christ};

Who opposes and exalts himself above all that is called God, or that is worshipped; so that he as God sits in the temple of God, showing himself that he is God.

Remember you not, that, when I was yet with you, I told you these things?

And now you know what will withhold that he might be revealed in his time.

<u>For the mystery of iniquity does already work</u>: only he who now lets (hinders) will let (hinder) {concerning Divine Destiny} until he is taken out of the way.

And then shall that Wicked be revealed, whom the {Master} lord shall consume with the spirit of his mouth, and shall destroy with the brightness of his coming:

Even him {Anti-christ}, whose coming is after the work of Satan, with all power and signs and lying wonders,

And with all deceivableness of unrighteousness in them that perish; <u>because they did not receive the love of truth, that they might be saved</u>.

<u>And for this cause, God will send them strong delusion</u> that they should believe a lie {follow the ways and dictates of this liar or the selfishness of their own souls}:

That they all might be damned who believed not the truth, but had pleasure in unrighteousness.

Paul's advice is most definitely Islamic when he declares:

Therefore, brothers, stand fast, and hold {to} the traditions {Sunnah} which you have been taught, whether by word or our epistle. 2 Thessalonians (2: 15)

This is good, sound advise and it tells the believer in any age to go back to the original source and to hold onto what is the life's blood of any religion and that is the practices of the one who was originally sent to keep man free from falling into the ditch of dogmatic error as well as providing a source to console the soul and to make the way clean and pure.

In the Gospel of John, Jesus (pbh) declares who and what he is as I have tried to explain in my two previous books, *The real Holy Grail: The Messiah on Trial and He is not My Ancestor.*

Muhammad (pbh) did the same. Why should these two prophets of world fame hide what and who they were? However, they both put these things in the proper perspective and were not arrogant or self-serving. They both declared that they were but men. Men who could not pluck a blade of grass if it were not for the Permission of their Lord and men having everything to fear if they turned away from their Lord and men having to depend upon their Lord for their very success in seeking salvation for themselves.

The problem for the Peoples of the Book has always been the consistency, coordination and perspective in understanding Divine Scripture. Whereas some become bloated by their own importance and see scripture as confirming their own excellence, others have taken a more practical approach in trying to understand harmony, unity and reality.

This mentality actually becomes a 'war' within side man's soul as to how he operates between various peoples and systems and how he treats or mistreats people. Such is the way men have kept toiling down through the ages.

So in the practical sense, most men are not really different than the pagan Arabs of old. Yes, we believe in a One God of sorts and yes, we believe in an afterlife of sorts but so didn't they. So what is the real difference between modern man and the pagan Arabs of old? In reality, there is not that much of a difference and that is very scary indeed!

APPENDIX A

THE ACTS OF THE APOSTLES

One of the best pieces of literature, which can clarify many misconceptions about Christianity, found in the New Testament is what purports to be a historical, capsulated version of the doings of early Christianity beginning after the Resurrection of Jesus the Christ (pbh). Modern day scholars have noted many flaws in this writing but are positive that it is a valuable piece of literature whose original author attempted to tell the truth according to his personal viewpoint as if being taught or trained by another. In other words, the supposed author does not claim divine inspiration by himself but tries to give an accurate reflection of the times he lived in as well as a personalized viewpoint from a certain sect to which he belonged. The author does not hide the fact that his partial influence and knowledge of events comes from one Paul of Tarsus or those familiar with Paul. In fact, the author claims that he was a sometime companion and therefore a learner from Paul.

Honest and well-read scholars have found flaws in the document called *The Acts of the Apostles*. Some of these flaws are minor while some are major and quite disturbing but at the same time prophetic in nature. Moreover, when one takes these major flaws in context with actual revealed religion, they show an understandable trend and the nature of men concerning both good and evil as to illuminating the truth versus those who would try to cover it up.

One of the flaws of this record is the title, *The Acts of the Apostles*. The title doesn't fit the work and therefore scholars have agreed that at some point in time an artificial title was stuck on to this historical record or if that record had a title, then the correct title is now lost. A second flaw in this piece of literature concerns the author. It is conjectured that the author's name is Luke and it is further conjectured by some that it is the Luke who produced the Gospel according to Luke. However that may be, there is no real strong evidence for this, i.e. that the writer of the Acts is Luke and there is little evidence that he is the one who was responsible for the production of the Gospel according to Luke. At a guess, his name could be Luke or a version of it but for a certainty, it is not known.

Perhaps the best guess about this unknown author is that he was of Greek origin and that he grew up in a pagan environment but that he had a very rational and inquisitive mind. The time of his conversion to the Way of Jesus is unknown. However, he was probably a quick learner and joined a 'study group' concerning the ways and examples of his newfound prophet. Being over abundantly blessed in his new faith and highly intelligent, with excellent zeal, he was advanced far enough in his beliefs to journey with Paul on some of his travels being both student and younger companion. In addition, he seems to have a bent towards history and being a second-generation believer and concerned about current disturbances happening to the 'faithful', he feels the need to document things lest they be lost. His major contribution to early 'church' history is his dedication to put things down in a historical/Biblical concept. This tells us that he was aware of the great tribulations (Fitna) affecting the body of believers and wanted to preserve important details that might become lost in the turmoil that was ongoing.

His claim of having written another work on the history of Jesus is probably accurate but that work, in all probability, did not survive. His first couple of chapters in the Acts is not about Paul but conveys some critical points after the Resurrection through the eyes of Peter who he never met. This shows that he had access to certain records, verbal or otherwise. As to the particular church (sect), he belonged to or ended up in, one cannot be certain. The result is that his life as well as his death remains a mystery to this day. That is not a good sign when one considers that such an exalted text forms a mainstay of the New Testament. His Acts was probably written somewhere in the late 70s to early 80s AC and he probably died or was murdered on or before 90 AC joining those who suffered for their faith.

Being an excellent historian and very perceptive of his faith, he could not help be aware of the horrendous threat that the followers of the Way were under. In fact, the carnage of the fall of Jerusalem, the butchering of many innocent people, the tendency of wolves in sheep's clothing to cause trouble and the Roman experience with their gods and love of the world would not have evaded him. Furthermore, he would have known the manner and times of death of both Peter and Paul. Yet his Acts ends with Paul in prison—house arrest. This is not a sign of a true historian—to leave things hanging in the air. Therefore, it seems that certain people of the second century did their own peculiar editing of this manuscript and the most logical thoughts about this would point to the Roman hierarchy at some point in time. Why?

They were the ones who finally ended up with the dominion and so the least amount of embarrassing questions asked the better. The same holds true today with some world leaders who fight against corruption but they themselves need not be questioned concerning such a trivial matter!

Besides these minor flaws, there are some major flaws of interesting proportions. One of the biggest flaws is set around 'just exactly' when this piece of literature was written. Various sources give 'credible' reasons for it to be produced between 64 AC to 120 AC and that by inference tells us to be very careful concerning its interpretation. However, the most acceptable non-fraudulent reasoning places this document between 75-85 AC. If this is so, then it becomes an extremely damaging document against certain thoughts held by a majority of modern day Christians.

If the above date is entertained to be more accurate than other versions, another major flaw appears to leap out at the 'believer' and that flaw becomes huge for several reasons. One reason occurs when understanding that this piece of scripture is historical in nature. The author of this piece neglected the awesome events of before and after the 70 AC massacre by the Romans and the change that was brought about as to the impact of life in the Holy Land and elsewhere has been seemingly ignored to be put in the realm of the totally insignificant.

The present day Acts, as was said before, ends with Paul's house arrest in Rome around 61-62 AC and seems like an incomplete document to say the least. So what does this show?

It shows quite simply a dangerous attempt by some authority to edit out crucial, historical information. Can that be proven? It most definitely can from some existent sayings in the Acts itself which in a broader context of comparative religion, clearly shows that some skullduggery was in the works.

The idea of using a 'broader context' is not farfetched because true scholars, no matter their religious preference, have already given their just opinion concerning the current New Testament. These individuals do not trash the New Testament but have in effect declared that the New Testament shows defects as to additions and subtractions, which although do not render the New Testament false, does at times give misleading and incomplete knowledge of what really took place.

Some people may take offence at this but those open and honest scholars are not denying the essentials of what people call 'Christianity' today. They are only, if not openly, denying the 100% perfection of the New Testament.

To give further credence to the above thoughts when one is looking at the specific history of Pope Linus and his successor Pope Anacletus whose combined reigns lasted about 24 years after the martyrdom of Peter the Apostle, one runs into an almost blank wall. This is important to note because during their reigns when Christianity was in its important developing stage, the most important times of 'church' history is just about blank.

In Islam, the history of the two Caliphs Abu Bakr and 'Umar, after the death of the Prophet (pbh), are fairly well documented. Books can be written about that era and several have. In contrast, the history of the two aforementioned popes and the crucial history that took place are invisible. Therefore, a great deal of treachery, double-dealings and the striving of protecting the Way of true faith are in reality absent.

What of the Acts and what can it tell us that is so damaging? Three things become very apparent when putting true history under the microscope—a history that many will not take kindly to. Two statements found in the Acts can show some surprising things when studying comparative religion:

- Partial exoneration of the man called Paul. This is not a major issue here. However, after finishing the next two points one must wonder why a proclaimed companion (follower and student) of Paul would make such statements if Paul were a corrupt liar.
- Statement # 1—Jesus is just a good man blessed by the God of all sons of Adam (none possess God) by miracles given to him from his Creator.
- Statement # 2—People must follow Prophet Muhammad (pbh). That is, that they must follow, listen to, hear, obey and believe all things he communicates to them or else they will be rejected!

It would be an amazing thing if the Acts talk about these things—but they do!

The first point concerning Paul has been dealt with in my previous books. If the author of the Acts is a true and honest man, then he certainly seems to give Paul some credit and even looks up to him as his <u>mentor</u>. It would only be logical to assume that the student appreciated his master and passed on accurately his personal recollections.

The second point is a lot easier to follow and a lot easier to understand until one runs into the crucifixion idea. However, that should pose no difficulty at all when two things are considered:

1. The third point that will be made concerning Islam and the following of 'That Prophet' as expressed in the Acts.
2. The fact that certain words or parts of words in the Bible have been criminally altered. Even certain words

have been substituted for original words will not be found to be unknown.

What all this means is that one has to take a very close look at the human experience—basically the war between the sons of darkness and the sons of light—and consider the third point to be presented which clearly shows Islam as the Way mentioned in the Acts as to the future truth.

Here is point two:

You men of Israel hear these words; Jesus of Nazareth, a man approved of God among you by miracles and wonders and signs, which God did by him in the midst of you, as you yourselves also know:
Him, being delivered by the determinate counsel and foreknowledge of God, you have taken, and by wicked hands have crucified and slain. ACTS (2: 22-23)

Here is ACTS (2: 23) as it should have appeared:

Him, being delivered by the determinate counsel and foreknowledge of God, you have taken, and by wicked hands have {SOUGHT} to crucify and slay. ACTS (2: 23)

The third point brings everything to a boil. It is the most important aspect of the Acts itself and is not in anyway insignificant. It concerns a raised up Jesus who has left the earth and as such, his mission is completed until he is permitted to return.

However, after him (Jesus) will come, according to the Acts, another Prophet who has to be followed, obeyed and listened to or else the people will die! Now everybody dies—both adherents and non-adherents to truth but this death is not talking about the physical death as much as it is talking about the spiritual death and punishment to those of the rebellious. In addition, the meaning of that verse is on more than one level of understanding.

One level of understanding is that spiritual death or damnation will occur to those who will oppose That Prophet related by both the Gospels and the Quran—Math (12: 31-32) and Quran Sura Al-Kauthar (Sura: 108).

Yet another meaning is that his (the enemies of Jesus) will be cutoff during the return of Jesus the son of Mary to the glorious reign that was promised him, as he will be given the power to vanquish the hypocrites during the paradise on Earth during the Fifth Age of man as he will follow the Quran and Sunnah of Prophet Muhammad (pbh).

Here is that verse with several previous verses given to provide <u>context</u>:

And He shall send Jesus Christ {again}, which before was preached unto you (Jews):

Whom <u>the heaven must receive until the times of restitution of all things</u>, which God has spoken by the mouth of all His holy prophets since the world began.

For Moses truly said unto the fathers, a Prophet shall the Lord your God raise up unto you of <u>your brethren</u>, <u>like unto me</u>; him shall you hear <u>in all things</u> whatsoever he shall say unto you.

And it shall come to pass, that <u>every soul</u>, which will <u>not hear That Prophet</u>, SHALL BE DESTROYED FROM AMONG THE PEOPLE. ACTS (3: 20-23).

From among 'your brethren' is an interesting piece of information. Historically, the Semitic peoples have two separate lines coming from the line of Abraham (pbh)—the line of Isaac (pbh) and the line of Ishmael (pbh). Jesus being the last of the 'Jewish Prophets' is the last of the line called the Isaac line. The words 'your brethren' therefore must by all logical definition be amongst the 'other' line or the Ishmael line which is considered today as the line called the Arab line.

A few Christian notables in the past have spoken that they knew very well that another prophet would come after Jesus and that this prophet would be from the Arab line. However, these notables gave no indication that he would come from Arabia. Historically, it seems that the thought of another prophet (kept very much secret from the going concern outside the priest-class) was going to come from the land now known as Syria.

The discussion of these verses together with a few other verses in the Old and New Testament shows without ambiguity who that new and expected Prophet will be. To deny these things for any reason, except for those mentally incapacitated, is a sign of pure ignorance and contempt. It cannot be hidden from men nor will it be hidden in the heavens and there is no place to hide or to pretend a cover-up. The ONE UNIVERSAL GOD, the God of all the creation and of humankind is not duped, tricked or outmaneuvered by His created things.

Frankly speaking, Jesus (pbh) was taken up to the heavens 40 days after his Passion according to *The Acts of the Apostles*. Therefore, the Jesus that was preached to 'them' has left the earth for several decades and won't come back until his much looked for SECOND COMING. Hence, when he comes, he will not declare that religion is out of vogue but will follow a BOOK, A WAY and A PRACTICE (SUNNAH). That particular book, way and practice will come from That Prophet who was sent after him or after his first coming into the world.

Because Jesus will follow those practices already established, it becomes crystal clear that those who do not hear (CONFORM TO THOSE PRACTICES, WAY AND THAT BOOK) will be 'DESTROYED FROM AMONG THE PEOPLE.' And this thought is further enhanced from Math. (13: 41-42):

The son of man shall send forth his angels, and they shall gather out of his kingdom all things that offend, and them which do iniquity;

And shall cast them into a furnace of fire: there shall be wailing and gnashing of teeth. Math (13: 41-42)

People can argue that the Arabs (but they are not the majority of Muslims) have woefully neglected their religion or do not perform according to its standards. Argue away but acknowledge the Pathway. Failure to do so puts the mirror on those who desire to define themselves as 'knowers' of His Word over even Himself. And even those who do this, even if they were to bring a ransom of a mountain of gold for their souls, it would not be accepted. Why? Does the Creator Lord feel poor or frightened by any worldly power? Or is it man's arrogance that becomes his 'god' or real lover. In any case, the turning towards the Real Reality is a prime requisite for salvation and not by gimmicks will man be saved.

An interesting sidebar to Acts (3: 20) comes from the words "Whom the heavens must receive until the times of restitution of all things ..." The meaning of this part of the verse is very deep and cannot be fully expressed in words alone because it deals in the mystery of what is called 'predestination' or Divine Destiny. However, the author of Acts does a great job in saying that Jesus (pbh) will stay in heaven until all things determined by Allah from His Divine Will have occurred. In other words, all restitution must occur before Jesus is allowed to come back. What does that mean?

Well, it wouldn't be easy to understand even if it could be put into words. This is so because of the **Divine Grace and Mercy** being put into play. Furthermore, there is the notion that every man is like the snowflake, alike but not one of them completely the same. A book that has tried to discuss this subject of Predestination and its meaning was written by 'Umar S. al-Ashqar and entitled, "*Divine Will and Predestination—In the Light of the Quran and Sunnah*—published by International Islamic Publishing House.

There are a few hadiths discussing this subject but two of them are very noteworthy:

the promise to Muhammad & death of the Anti-Christ.

Thauban reported that Allah's Messenger (pbh) said, "Allah drew the ends of the world near to one another for my sake. And I have seen its eastern and western ends. And the dominion of my Ummah would reach those ends which have been drawn near to me and I have been granted the red and the white treasures and I begged my Lord for my Ummah that it should not be destroyed because of famine, nor dominated by an enemy who is not amongst them to take their lives and destroy them root and branch, and My Lord said, "Muhammad, whenever I make a decision, there is none to change it. Well, I grant you for your Ummah that it would not be destroyed by famine and it would not be dominated by an enemy who would not be amongst it and would take their lives and destroy them root and branch even if all the people from the different parts of the world join hands together (for this purpose), but it would be amongst them, viz. your Ummah, that some people would kill others or imprison the others." (Sahih Muslim)

The second hadith, which is lengthy and has been shortened for brevity sake, also shows the idea of predestination:

Abu Huraira reported Allah's Messenger (pbh) as saying, "The Last Hour would not come until the Romans would land at al-A'maq or in Dabiq. An army of the best (soldiers) of the people of earth at that time will come from Medina (to counteract them)... Certainly, the time of prayer shall come and then Jesus (pbh) son of Mary would descend and would lead them in prayer. When the enemy of Allah (the Anti-christ) would see him (Jesus), it (he) would (disappear) just as the salt dissolves itself in water and if he (Jesus) were not to confront them (the enemy) at all, even then it (the enemy) would dissolve completely, but Allah would kill them by his hand and he would show them their blood on his lance (the lance of Jesus Christ)." (Sahih Muslim)

As Muslims, we know that Prophet Muhammad (pbh) has great honor with Allah and that his station is exceedingly high concerning the rest of the creation although of course he is just a man. So why would Allah not fulfill all of the Prophet's requests? It is quite simple. Allah had a Plan from the beginning—even before the foundations of the world were in place. What is decided is to be and Allah will not alter the Perfect Plan from His Design for any reason simply because an altered plan would show that the original plan was defective in someway and that would reflect that somehow the Perfect Planner was not Perfect. Therefore, in showing His Greatness, He refuses even His Prophet sent to all of mankind.

This has an implication that amongst the people, (Muhammad's Nation) in particular when referring to the above hadith, restitution must be made whole and complete even when we as humans do not understand how, why, where, when and what. This restitution is similar to the saying, "If I catch you out in something, it will eventually boomerang on me and I will be caught out in something like what I did to you."

In order to accomplish this feat, one is forced to look upon Allah in awesome amazement, as it would require an Essence far and above what humankind and all of the creation could hope to conceive of as to His Power, Dominance, Might and Wisdom. Hence, we know of Allah and about Him only that which He permits us to know and never could there be any thought or question that He would have a partner or someone to compare unto Him. Far above is He to be contained or controlled yet He is closer to mankind than their own neck vein.

One can see how the greatness of men, and there have been great men, like the greatness of Moses, Jesus and Muhammad have stirred the hearts and minds of their respective followers. Yet when it came to true worship, these great men prostrated in the dust to that One they served without question and in fear and awe.

So as to the sector of the human race called the Arabs in relationship to the hadith just presented, the meaning is that you will be paid back as you have paid others and that is a good reason to accept one's consequences but in hope rather than fear. For even the New Testament declares that whatever a man meets out the same will be meted out to him.

As to how these things are accomplished and the degree of severity or the lack thereof is not known by any man so why should man try to fathom what he cannot fathom? Rather the wisest thing to do is to worship the One Who holds all things in His Hands in truth.

As to the death of the Anti-Christ, it has been recorded before his creation so what is so amazing about that? Yes, the Messiah will kill him but the importance of this rather lengthy hadith shows that with the Messiah or without him, the Anti-Christ will still come to his end that has been predestined for him. In this way of thinking, it becomes important to remember that it is God Who is the Fashioner of all things and is in Control of all things and that His Dominance and Power are far, far above what mankind could attribute to Him.

Another lesson to learn from this is that Islam does not practice or believe in 'fatalism' although many in the West, who do not have a very good distinction between Planning versus fatalism, have called it that. The distinctions between a fine-tuned Plan and fatalism seem to be very tenuous to many people and that is normal because it would take a great deal of time and effort to go into this philosophical argument, which is not in most people's benefit to do. Therefore, the book of 'Umar S. al-Ashqar was mentioned as it should suffice in that area. People have been requested to go to the spirit of truth to find out about the truth and this is not a new thing as Jesus himself, as is recorded in the present day Gospels, requested it.

Some people might ask, "When were these thoughts concerning the coming of a new prophet lost in historic times?" It would be difficult if not impossible to come to a definitive answer. A hard look at Christian history shows several 'dark' periods where vital knowledge is missing. The best evidence so far, which is admittedly spotty, shows several things.

There is no general trend after 100 AC that is known that shows any major evidence for a strong remembrance of another Prophet to come after Jesus. It is true that there arose many different sects concerning Jesus of Nazareth. It is also true that a formalized version of 'true' Christianity did not appear until around about 130 AC. It is also true that one of Paul's favorite 'churches', the Corinthians, were one of the last to hold out for the non-crucifixion of Jesus. Finally, it is true that the formation of a real coordinated New Testament of some sorts came around 170 AC. So what can be made of this?

It would appear that through martyrdom and generation dilution, as to true knowledge of the faith, the idea of a new Prophet to arise became lost in the shuffle (out of sight, out of mind) as an important issue somewhere around 100 AC. A few sects probably held on to that idea as a major tenant of belief but because of Fitna (turmoil) spoken by Jesus, John (16: 33) caused so much trouble along with the 'wolves in sheep's clothing' or corrupt spiritual guides, the knowledge of a new Prophet became reduced to a trivial matter.

In addition, since there were no printing presses at that time, various sects were like islands in a strong sea being eroded by all sorts of foolish notions. Hence, the philosophical nonsense, which engulfed the church later, could easily bury the situation under the guise of running after the total foolishness of trying to cut open the Christ and see how many natures he had!

The declaration of Acts (3: 20-23) is important for two reasons. First, it gives testimony for those who desire salvation to take heart that the One God did not leave His 'people' who He cared for in a defenseless position. His people are not defined, as being a race or nation, but those whom He has chosen from the beginning and that knowledge is with Him alone! He is the One Who possess and owns. Nobody, no person, race or religion owns, dictates or sets limits to Him. Therefore, there is no chosen people per say but there is a chosen Way which is judged solely by Him as laid down through the institution He created—the one brotherhood of prophets. These prophets were not sent to force humanity against its will but to enlist 'helpers' and loyalists of these prophets in surrender to the One God and His Will.

The second reason clearly shows that there will be another Prophet <u>after</u> Jesus. Why must this be so?

Why should another Prophet be sent and what is his purpose? Prophets are not sent to the obedient peoples because they come to instruct, purify and teach that knowledge which is lost or twisted and bring a cleaned remembrance back to the Creator Lord as He Wills it. When, however, a special Prophet is sent to all of humanity, this symbolizes that humanity is to be discussed as a collective whole. That is, that the Last Hour is NOW and that the paradise on earth as well as the Last Day of Judgment is somewhere in the future. Moreover, being the last Prophet sent gives humanity a warning that is clear and unambiguous. It also gives people a chance to refresh and renew their commitment to their Creator Lord.

However, people who are in the grip of being 'asleep' as the New Testament declares or those who are under the spell of a corrupt priest-class (willingly or unwillingly) cannot seem to grasp the logic of these things and therefore are divided and held back from seeing the obvious. If only they took more time to study the scriptures and ask for awareness, perhaps they might come to a realization of truth and harmony between people of good faith.

But lo! What has been set in motion from the beginning of time has to be completed to separate the wheat from the chaff and to complete the restitution of all things. That is one reason the Believer is asked to pray in earnest for His Grace, Mercy and Forgiveness in sincerity. And He is going to be the Judge of who is sincere and who is only pretending to be sincere. Therefore, no one can escape His Perfect net and He will collect the 'fish' and separate them as He Decides and no one will be able to argue with Him.

A person covered in slime is as a person covered in worldly affairs. If he remembers to take a bath, so much the better for him as he goes out to meet his betters. The same holds for his soul and what that person presents to his Creator Lord. This is not done overnight but if one truly remembers Him, He will not forget that person.

APPENDIX B

THE PAULINE CONTROVERSY

The Pauline controversy just adds fuel to the fire unless it is understood. And how many people can understand this man and the times he was in? Once again, it is mandatory to go back to the original sources and if possible the original language of the prophetic scriptures but for the vast majority of people that is not practical. Therefore, it becomes a primary importance to take in all of the scripture with an understanding of Divine Unity and the knowledge that the One God is for all peoples and for all times if they would but accept it!

Here are some excerpts from one of my books entitled, *The Islamic Messiah* which hopefully will make the position concerning Paul a little bit more understandable.

Saul becomes Paul

With murder, prison and double dealings with the Roman authorities holding strong, a seed gets planted which turns into a rock sent hurdling toward a pond. The ripples made by this rock (Paul) still reverberate to this day. This man didn't start out like a firecracker but he ended up being a fuse that took the fledgling 'church' into two directions: upwards an onwards and also spiraling downwards. And the joy of it is, it can be proven!_

Saul held the whip hand and hurt the new Jews badly. Sometime after his persecutions of the people of the new Way he becomes Paul. He now becomes a traitor to the majority of Jews, a regular turncoat, who espouses the new Way after his claimed spiritual growth and enlightenment. His relationship to old Judaism is severed and he becomes a new found Jew in the Messiah and after a decade or so, he will be hitting hard and fast. He becomes the bee with a stinger in Jewish history and a man so hated that attempts were made on his life as well as being stuck in prison for several years at various times. So ends the enigmatic story of Paul. Ends???

Well, he lit fires all over the place that make various people dizzy and yes at times confused. Only by going to the spirit of truth can we even hope to gain a foothold into this complex individual.

It is peculiar that Prophet Muhammad (pbh) had said things similar to what Paul said but of course in greater detail and with more depth of meaning. Most Muslims might feel terribly perplexed about this or even angry but it is the truth and will be presented eventually, Allah Willing.

To understand Paul is a terrible task. If a psychologist were to read his 'so-called' writings, he would get an important clue. Frankly, his 'writings' seem to come from a man suffering a mild form of schizophrenia. That is an important clue. To understand this, one has to go into church history. Church history is another garbled jewel all by itself. However, let us now know that at certain times the so-called Pauline Epistles were numbered at 13. Nowadays, when people who are experts in analyzing scripture review Paul's work, they have come to a determination that Paul may have written only 6 or 7 of those epistles. Upon further review by experts in the field, Paul may be credited with only parts of these epistles.

Before Paul disappears altogether from the New Testament, let us look at things from a new perspective with more insight.

All 13 epistles credited at various times to Paul have what is called a Pauline-like flavor. Some of those epistles (and this cannot be proven) were re-worked as late as 110 AD or nearly half a century after his death. It cannot be proven because no one can find the originals to carbon date them.

The proof for this is found in the writing structures and points of view presented. Not only was Pauline-type Christianity favorable to the idea of 'to the Jew first', it also shows that after this philosophy is given and was rejected by the Jews for the most part, it then becomes a philosophy of 'you had your chance and now it is time to move on' to the gentiles or non-Jew.

Something else is also shown within these documents when history is looked into more closely. It shows that competing Pauline 'churches' did tend to compete with each other in presenting their viewpoints. In other words, you may be a Paulist but you are a poor Paulist as compared to our sect—the 'real' Paulist or followers of Paul.

This competitive nonsense is nothing but sectarianism and a rethinking of Paul to present favorable viewpoints concerning one's specialized sect is rather damaging not to mention highly illegal and a misuse of faith.

And We granted them clear Signs in Affairs (of Religion—the correct pathway of belief and behavior): it was only <u>after</u> knowledge had been granted to them that they fell into schisms, through <u>insolent envy among themselves</u>

(arrogant hairsplitting). Verily thy Lord will judge between them on the Day Of Judgment as to those matters in which they set up differences. Q (45:17)

First of all there is no such thing as Pauline Christianity as was mentioned in one of my earlier books. It is just a sham and a cover-up basically used to present certain kinds of artificial philosophies. Paul existed but he never covered up the glory of the Messiah with his supposed brilliance and that is proven by the *Acts of the Apostles* as well as Paul's own true words when and if they can be found.

Now this idea is bound to cause a stir. Damaging evidence proving this does not just have to come from the New Testament. It can come from Islamic history as once again patterns can be seen to be repeating themselves. Forgery and guile are not a racial thing or limited to certain times or nations. Forgery and guile is an attempt in any age to color the truth and create bizarre twists of fiction into supposed eternal truths. Just looking at other faiths and their wondrous but ludicrous inventions can tell us that.

Thus have We placed leaders in every town, its wicked men, to plot (and burrow) therein: but they only plot against their own souls, and they perceive it not.

Q (6:123)

For I know this, that after my departing shall grievous wolves enter in among you, not sparring the flock.

Also of your own selves shall men arise, speaking perverse things, to draw away disciples after them. Acts (20:29-30)

And account that the longsuffering of our Lord is salvation; even as our beloved brother Paul also according to the wisdom given unto him has written unto you;

As also in all his epistles, speaking in them of these things; in which are some things <u>hard</u> to be understood, which they that are <u>unlearned</u> and <u>unstable</u> wrest, as they do also the other scriptures, unto their own destruction.

You therefore, beloved, seeing you know these things before; <u>beware</u> lest you also, being led away with the error of the wicked, fall from your own steadfastness.

II Peter (3:15-17)

There arose during Paul's time various controversies concerning the Way. Basically, people were the believers who followed the Way and this notion preceded the idea of the name 'Christianity' as the formalized name for the sect of the Messiah.

And the same time there arose <u>no small stir about that way</u>. Acts (19:23)

So, about 15 years after the Resurrection of the Master, there arose controversies within side this new Jewish group concerning the ideas and ideals of the faith. These controversies were largely due to the fact of to the Jews first. But that idea was being altered by the conversion of gentiles into the 'church'. Actually there was no real church at that time but that expression was used to denote the body of believers. The gentiles that came into the belief of the Way were being put down as <u>second class</u> believers and that didn't set well with Paul.

Paul eventually made his way to Jerusalem where he had some minor confrontations with Peter and James. However, due to Paul's strong arguments that people should not be confined and regulated as second class citizens because of their birth and because if they really desired the truth, then they should be given some slack instead of held back as second class believers. His argument with Peter about not eating with the gentile converts because they were only gentiles shows that Peter was doing things contrary to the 'spirit' of the law of the new Way. Besides, why should the gentiles be treated differently when 'to the Jews first' was not going to be an eternal commandment?

In effect then there was granted something like a two-track system of Jewish converts and gentile converts to the new Way. At this time Pharisaical Judaism was not dead but very much alive and would continue to be a thorn in the way of the new Judaism that was emerging and that would mean these two philosophies would have to coexist but under very uneasy terms with hanky-panky not being eliminated. Pharisaical Judaism was to exist for some more years until the second great civil war led by their false messiah—Simon Bar Kokhba who eventually was killed in 135 AD and Judaism has never really recovered since that time. It is estimated that over a half million Jews lost their lives in this civil war and that many Jews were eventually dispersed throughout many lands leading to what they call the great Diaspora.

The importance of this war is that the new Jewish sect, which had been badly mistreated by the old one, refused to join in on this war against Rome as was the case of the first civil war (70AD). But this was based on a religious policy of acceptance of 'those in leadership put over you' and not because they were afraid of the Romans. So, by 135 AD the Jewish religion was in disarray and as historically proven has never come to dominate the world scene as they had done before. The new Jews with the gentiles filling up their ranks would now take center stage as a major religious philosophy and would eventually become known far and wide as

Christians. They too took on the responsibility of the Divine Message but they wrangled about philosophy and therefore they fell down also. Q (5: 14) Taken from the book, *The Islamic Messiah* pages 30-35.

Behold! Allah said: "O Jesus! I will take you and raise you to Myself and clear you (of the falsehoods) of those who blaspheme; Q (3: 55)

Every man must have his 'day in court' to account for his actions and will be found acceptable or not acceptable for salvation. This also applies to Jesus because in truth he is only a man. But if he is already cleared from being one of the contemptible ones and raised up with great honor Q (3: 45) then that is a form of judgment allowing him to don the form of excellence of creation of man's purified and exalted standard—a Vicegerent. Therefore, when he returns, he returns with the power and dignity given to him as a ruler or commander of the faithful. Hence, he does not return as a weakling or a pushover but as one who has achieved great dominion because of his excellent servitude to His Way.

It is such as obey Allah and His Messenger, and fear Allah and do right, that will triumph.
Q (24: 52)

As to descending from heaven, pouring amazing wealth from his hands, slaying the anti-christ and being able to slay any hypocrite with his breath as far as his eyes can see well that is part of the job and part of his power that is given him. Why can't a man who has received judgment and is held in high honor as a Vicegerent do these things? He certainly is judged as a high level of creation and mere atoms of matter are not going to frighten him. So the fortunate ones alive during that era will see him as he really is and how he worships his Lord with strict devotion.

What is the truth about this Islamic Messiah known as Jesus the son of Mary? As a man he is a leader among souls belonging to the Way. And as we have seen declared in the New Testament one of his future followers (Paul) was formerly engaged against the people who belonged to the Way.

Now Saul, still breathing threats and murder against the disciples of the Lord, went to the high priest, and asked for letters from him to the synagogues at Damascus, so that if he found any belonging to the Way, both men and women, he might bring them bound to Jerusalem. Acts (9: 1-2)

That is very succinctly put. It mentions not a named creed but of those who belong to a belief system called the Way which could be translated as the universal belief system of the faithful in any age who seek out truth over folly, live lives according to the tenants given by the prophets and who worship the One God in peace and surrender to His Will. That of course does not imply that they are perfect or without sin but implies those who are on the 'straight path' without trying to deviate from it. Hence, the sinner is **redeemed** because there is placed a light in his heart whereas the other sinner condemns himself because there is no light put in his heart (in that special place where no man knows).

... For any to whom Allah gives not light, there is no light! Q (24: 40)

The truth about the Messiah becomes crystal clear in the Quran minus all the fanciful falsehoods produced by divergent philosophies. So the Quran makes it clear, plain, simple and unambiguous. Philosophies are one thing but if they stray away from the truth and create divergent speculations, then they are useless. This is especially the case in dealing with 'religious' records because of the very nature of these records.

Once again the records of the People of the Book are not to be trifled with. However, they can be looked at as universal guidance systems giving man the roadmap to salvation. In looking at their universal 'truths' it becomes apparent that certain patterns are universal amongst men. For example, the saying, "You blind guides, which strain at a gnat, and swallow a camel Matt (23: 24) carries the same message as the following hadith:

'Abdullah reported Allah's Messenger (may peace be upon him) as saying: Ruined were those who indulged in hair-splitting. He (the Holy Prophet) repeated this three times. (Sahih Muslim)

Another example of universal activity comes from these words attributed to Paul:

For I know this, that after my departing shall grievous wolves <u>enter in among you</u>, not sparring the flock.

Also of your own selves shall men arise, <u>speaking perverse things</u>, to <u>draw away disciples</u> after them. Acts (20:29-30)

In all honesty one can see how all truthful religions have been affected by so-called crooked intellectuals who have tried their hand at inventing falsehoods while trying to propagate them as 'eternal' truths. But if one is careful and seeks understanding, then that person is less likely to be trapped by these false delusions that run contrary to the truth.

The best way of looking at the Messiah is through the last Revelation: the Quran.

And We made the son of Mary and his mother as a Sign ... Q (23: 50)

So in effect he was as well as his mother a Sign to mankind. It is not required for anyone to be able to define what kind of a Sign but to just know that he was a Sign.

Christ the son of Mary was no more than a messenger; many were the messengers that passed away before him. His mother was a woman of truth. They had both to eat their (daily) food. See how Allah does make His Signs clear to them; yet see in what ways they are deluded away from the truth. Q (5: 75)

Jesus (pbh) was a messenger and of course a man. It is not a pre-requirement of faith to debate on what kind of messenger or man he was.

These were the men to whom We gave the Book and the Judgment and Prophethood: if these (their descendents) reject them, Behold! We shall entrust their charge to a new people who reject them not. Q (6: 89)

A veiled threat? If a person rejects their way, then he is also rejected. If that appears to be a new idea, it is not.

Verily, verily, I say unto you, he that enters not by the door into the sheepfold, but climbs up <u>some other way</u>, the same is a thief and a robber. John (10:1)

How well does one understand the terms thief and robber? Is it that some are born lucky? The answer is definitely not! The answer goes to the heart of what religion is or what it is meant to convey—any religion. So the saying "but climbs up some other way, the same is a thief and a robber" conveys the contest of wills. There is His Will and there are the individuals soul's will. Therefore, the soul is given the chance to surrender to His Will rather than going off on a tangent and doing its will. Those doing that declare that 'my will' is superior to His Will or I make the rules and He (God) will follow them. Taken from the book, *The Islamic Messiah* pages 93-96.

CONCLUSION

The overemphasis for the importance of the crucifixion or death of Jesus (pbh) on the cross was not put in place until the era of Constantine. Historically, the issue of whether Jesus was or was not on the cross and crucified was settled around 148 AC according to the Roman church's satisfaction. In addition, the idea of Jesus being crucified was believed by certain Jewish-Christian sects for various reasons from the time of the actual crucifixion event. Furthermore, the declaration that Jesus rose from the dead was bound to cause trouble to those who lacked a deep comprehension in religious matters. The reasons for the above appear to be varied.

Before the actual formation of Christianity as a distinct religious movement, several ideas were floating around and one of them was that Jesus was not of the 'flesh' but a spiritual being. To counteract that idea, the notion that Jesus was actually crucified took shape as if to prove his real existence and that he was not just an 'angelic' figure but a real person.

What one can see here is an 'evolutionary' process that shows a great deal of disrespect and tomfoolery of all sorts pervading the issue.

The best people to know about these dramatic events and the best people to know the importance of these events and their relationship to the truth are not the half-baked philosophers, the false Gnostics or the hand-kissing sycophants who lacked depth when it came to the study of religion. The best people who knew the truth of these things were Jesus (pbh) and his devoted Companions.

In truth, there is not much we can get from that category because Jesus has been raised up and his Companions have been dead for almost two-thousand years. In the intervening years there have been some developments, however, that would help to make the issue clear.

Some may ask, "How is it that two physical bodies are in the grave but only one comes out?" It is not given to man to chase after mysteries but to live in and by faith. However, perhaps a partial solution to that problem can be found.

How is it possible that a flesh and blood Jesus (pbh) could enter into the 'safe' house that the Companions were hiding in if he did not come through the door or a window? Obviously, he did not stand outside the house and knock on the door saying, "Guess who this is. Will you please let me in?" Therefore, how can two solid objects come into contact with each other (his body and the wall) and he overcomes the wall?

We do know from scriptures that his Companions were afraid when they saw him and they thought that he either was a spirit or a devil because they asked him a favor (to ask his LORD to send a Table set with food) to demonstrate that he was for real and that he was actually flesh and bones and also that he was telling the truth and not a liar.

In the New Testament, Jesus is also challenged to perform a function on himself as in:

And he (Jesus) said to them, "You will surely say to me this proverb", 'Physician, heal thy self: whatsoever we have heard done in Capernaum, do also here in your country'. Luke (4: 23)

That is to say that you (querulous people) are telling me about the signs that I have been given from my LORD to perform and that you see with your own eyes that if I am the one who I am (the real Messiah) that I have to perform that what I do on myself or else you won't believe!!! Read that verse again and again to sense its meaning.

So the question is, "How could two bodies become one?" is like asking how can a body enter through a solid wall? Or it is like asking, "How could Prophet Muhammad (pbh) in one night make a journey from Arabia to Jerusalem and then ascend up to the 7 levels of heaven and back down again and return to Arabia in less than a day?" Or perhaps it is asking, "How could Jesus walk on water and multiply the loaves and fishes or how could Prophet Muhammad (pbh) crack the moon in half?"

The answer is simple. For those who have faith let them have faith and for those who are querulous, let them be querulous. Or perhaps the saying of Paul could be used here:

For the mystery of iniquity does already work: only he who now lets (hinders) will let (hinder), until he be taken out of the way. 2 Thess. (2: 7)

A scriptural issue is best dealt with by the scripture as a whole and understanding scripture in its context. Also, prophetic forces must come into play in this highly logical system because the nature of a prophet is to come and deliver stark reality and not shifty irrelevancies. Hence, in order to be non-biased one must find a hook to hang one's proverbial hat or else forego the discussion as being irrelevant and immaterial.

Since it is not preferred to dwell among those whose religious comprehension is minimal at best, the only pathway to use is scripture and scriptural analysis as a first line of defense.

Pulling out a few verses of scripture is generally unreasonable in trying to build a solid case because those verses may not cover the story in full. Furthermore, those verses may be interpreted incorrectly or interpreted as one wants to see them interpreted. In addition, one has to be careful of the translation of these verses from the original language as well as making sure that those verses actually are pure in content. The task is a daunting one for those belonging to one's school of thought and becomes even more daunting when looked at in a comparative religious viewpoint.

However, there are several verses that do present a challenge to the People of the Book to clarify the issue.

One of these verses is found in **Acts (3: 20-23)** and presents a huge challenge to the logic of man. These verses are clear and unambiguous in the declaration of a prophet of Arab descent who will come after Jesus. This prophet will be extremely essential so much so that the 'spiritual' life of the person not following 'his Way' will be forfeited at a certain unspecified time during the return of Jesus (pbh). In these particular verses, the name of That Prophet is not mentioned nor is the direct connection between the 'spiritual' death occurring from not listening to him (following his ways) given a timeframe. Why should it be given in those verses?

Scriptural verses are not thrown up for the thoughtless or heedless but for those who make an attempt at understanding. After all, the name of Jesus was not mentioned in the Old Testament as the one who would come and be the Messiah but a person has to truly work for that and see the signs of his coming. And this idea was also laid out in the Six Ages of man theory presented in my former writings which show a continuation and a consistency of truth down through the ages.

With this consistency and an understanding of the need for openness and transparency, it has become clear that the People of the Book have various agendas of their own and would prefer not to discuss the above verses in a logical and rational way. However, why then blame the Pharisees for baiting Jesus (pbh) and **asking for yet another sign**? It must therefore be as the Master said and that is "that it is an evil and adulterous generation that asks for a sign." That is, that it is evil to keep asking for repeated signs when it is clear that the evidence is pointing in an unmistakable direction and that these signs are cast away as if they meant nothing.

As to the soul what can one say? A simple demonstration might bring the soul into perspective. If a person were to stand next to a hydrogen bomb as it was exploding, his body would be instantly vaporized. However, his soul would not die. There is no force or forces capable of destroying a man's soul in the entire universe.

However, there is One Who can destroy it and this can be done as simply as He made it—such a thing is easy for Him and well within His grasp.

The point being made is that all due respect and homage is due to Him Who is far above the notion of having partners joined with Him. Why mix the leaven with the lump? Worship is for Him alone and not for any of His servants. That is the Reality and that is the truth.

It has been written in the Quran that believers should make no 'distinctions' between the prophets and that is true. Of course there are the understandable distinctions of size, race, language, customs, gifts, birthplace, etc but the distinction mentioned here is one of relevancy. All of the prophets were human beings, sons of Adam and belonged to a unified body of truth serving One God while belonging to a system called the Way (Islam) in English.

And whoever seeks a religion other than Islam, it will not be accepted of him, and in the Hereafter he will be one of the losers. Q (3: 85)

Each prophet that came to mankind is like an essential brick in a building (the Way) made from those bricks. They have been measured, weighed and put in place by that BUILDER Who, as Master Planner, perfected all and designed all things. And His Plan had depth, scope and purpose such that none of the creation could fathom it save Himself. And when mankind came into being, he too was part of the Perfect Plan as it slowly unfolded and as men went their divergent ways into a near infinite number of niches, so also the Plan was there proving that He Alone knew what was before and in front of man. Such is His Glory and His Greatness.

But man is a contentious lot at times and wants to go his own way and be dominating at that. There are some who would try to force others to worship inanimate objects or even carbon-based life forms as in other men. There are some who do not force but delight in worshiping carbon-based life forms that eat and excrete but who accomplish wonderful deeds. This is nothing more than a disease of the heart and perhaps a longing for self-same recognition.

To put it succinctly as the noblest of souls, Yusef (pbh) put it:

"And I follow the ways of my fathers—Abraham, Isaac, and Jacob; and never could we attribute any partners whatever to Allah: that (comes) of the Grace of Allah to us and to mankind: yet most men are not grateful.

"O my companions of the prison (I ask you): Are many lords differing among themselves better, or the One, Supreme and Irresistible?

"Whatever you worship apart from Him is nothing but names which you have named, you and your fathers, for which Allah has sent down no authority. The Command is for none but Allah. He has commanded that you worship none but Him. That is the Right Religion, but most men understand not ..." Q. (12: 38-40)

www.ingramcontent.com/pod-product-compliance
Ingram Content Group UK Ltd.
Pitfield, Milton Keynes, MK11 3LW, UK
UKHW021053270726
13967UKWH00012B/644

9 781425 180805